The Cruise of
the Corwin

The John Muir Library

The Story of My Boyhood and Youth
A Thousand-Mile Walk to the Gulf
My First Summer in the Sierra
The Yosemite
The Mountains of California
The Cruise of the Corwin
Travels in Alaska
Our National Parks

JOHN MUIR

The Cruise of the Corwin

SIERRA CLUB BOOKS · SAN FRANCISCO

The Sierra Club, founded in 1892 by John Muir, has devoted itself to the study and protection of the earth's scenic and ecological resources—mountains, wetlands, woodlands, wild shores and rivers, deserts and plains. The publishing program of the Sierra Club offers books to the public as a nonprofit educational service in the hope that they may enlarge the public's understanding of the Club's basic concerns. The point of view expressed in each book, however, does not necessarily represent that of the Club. The Sierra Club has some sixty chapters coast to coast, in Canada, Hawaii, and Alaska. For information about how you may participate in its programs to preserve wilderness and the quality of life, please address inquiries to Sierra Club, 730 Polk Street, San Francisco, CA 94109.

Foreword copyright © 1993 by Roderick Nash

Library of Congress Cataloging-in-Publication Data
Muir, John, 1838–1914.
   The cruise of the Corwin / John Muir.
     p.   cm.
   Originally published : Boston : Houghton Mifflin, 1917.
   Includes index.
   ISBN 0-87156-523-4
     1. Arctic regions—Discovery and exploration.   2. Corwin (Ship)
I. Title.
[G625.M85   1993]
919.8—dc20   92-25139
                                                    CIP

Production by Susan Ristow
Book design and illustration by Michael McCurdy
Map by Hilda Chen
Composition by Wilsted & Taylor

Printed in the United States of America on acid-free paper containing a minimum of 50% recovered waste paper of which at least 10% of the fiber content is post-consumer waste

10   9   8   7   6   5   4   3   2   1

Contents

Contents

Foreword

In the Spring of 1881, when the *Corwin* began a voyage of 15,000 nautical miles into Arctic seas, John Muir's life was in transition and so was America's. For Muir the 1880s marked the end of two decades of wandering in the wilderness and the beginning of a settled family existence. Between 1880, when he was 42, and 1886, Muir got married, fathered two daughters and plunged into a new career as gentleman farmer. Never again would he pursue what he called "the old lonely life," the description of which was such an important factor in early American wilderness appreciation. Henceforth Muir would devote himself to his children, his orchards and his publications, and to defending the wilderness he had come to love. But suddenly in 1881 an opportunity arose for a last great wilderness hurrah!

The *Corwin* was a sail and steam ship in the employ of the United States Revenue Cutter Service, now known as the Coast Guard. Captained by Calvin L. Hooper, it had several specific objectives in 1881. The most dramatic from the standpoint of public attention was a search for George Washington De Long and his ship *Jeannette*, which had left San Francisco two years earlier in a questionable effort to drift across the North Pole while trapped in pack ice. There had been no word from the expedition for months. The *New York Herald*, a financial backer of De Long, was clamoring for a search and rescue mission and also undoubtedly relishing the prospect of reporting a sensational encounter at the ends of the earth in the manner of Stanley and Livingstone. In addition, Captain Hooper had orders to check on compliance with interna-

Foreword

tional seal- and otter-hunting covenants and to investigate the disappearance of two American whaling ships. Finally the *Corwin* was to look into the condition of the starving natives of St. Lawrence Island just south of the Bering Strait.

John Muir's agenda in 1881 was different and, in a sense, more complicated. He was fascinated by glaciers. His reports on glaciation in the Yosemite region began his literary career, and in 1879 Muir explored the spectacular tidewater glaciers of Southeast Alaska. Calvin Hooper's invitation to board the *Corwin* was an opportunity to study the effect of ice on land still further north. Arctic botany was a secondary scientific interest. But I suspect Muir's most powerful motivation stemmed from his perception that the American frontier was vanishing. This was, of course, a subset of a broader trend: the great age of European discovery and exploration was almost over. Real wilderness was disappearing rapidly from the planet. Cruising on the *Corwin* meant a chance to visit one of the world's last unexplored coastlines. Muir had been several generations behind the explorers of California and the West. In the North he could still be in the vanguard. Moreover, Muir could also make what we would today call a statement about his personal freedom. There is considerable evidence that he took up the responsibilities of marriage, family, and farming with mixed emotions. His early life had been the essence of wildness and freedom. Was he becoming tied down in his fourth decade? Six months at sea (possibly a year if the *Corwin* over-wintered in the ice) might be understood as an expression of middle-aged rebellion.

Most readers will find the highlight of *The Cruise of the Corwin* to be Muir's account of the so-called discovery of Wrangel

Foreword

Island north and west of the Bering Strait which occurred on August 12, 1881. As modern attitudes toward the abilities of native people and Anglo-European patronization change, a subject of some concern is the authenticity of such discoveries. Was Hooper's landing party, Muir included, really the first to set foot on Wrangel? Let us recognize at the outset that Wrangel is quite large (about 2,500 square miles) and relatively close (85 miles) to the Asian continent. It was well within the reach of the natives' larger skin boats such as the *umiak*. Remember, too, that the nautical skills of the Arctic natives were extraordinary. For thousands of years they had routinely paddled great distances across the North Pacific Ocean and the Bering Sea. Wrangel Island would have been a long one-day trip. Or they could have reached it over the pack ice as reindeer herds did. To his credit Muir takes seriously Chukchi traditions concerning passages to and even inhabitation of Wrangel. But nonetheless there he was on August 12, 1881 with the landing party, planting the American flag and claiming the unknown land for the United States. Both Russia and the United States claim the island today.

The book before you is one that Muir's literary executor, William F. Badè, pieced together from newspaper correspondence, published scientific articles and unpublished journals. It is not as polished as Muir's Sierra essays and the books published under his own supervision. Much of the text is matter-of-fact reporting with little of the philosophical content that distinguishes Muir's best work. But *The Cruise of the Corwin* tingles with the excitement of far and little-known horizons. In this respect Muir was writing in 1881 from the same perspective as Lewis and Clark in 1805 and John Wesley Powell in 1869. The critical difference was that Muir's

Foreword

account dealt with the closing chapters of North American frontier history. Whether he knew it or not at the time, the *Corwin* trip also concluded Muir's wilderness wandering.

Roderick Frazier Nash
1993

Introduction

One of the poignant tragedies of north polar exploration, that of the Jeannette, still lingers in the memory of persons now living, though a generation has since passed away. John Muir, who joined the first search expedition dispatched from San Francisco, had already achieved distinction by his glacial studies in the Sierra Nevada and in Alaska. The Corwin expedition afforded him a coveted opportunity to cruise among the islands of Bering Sea and the Arctic Ocean, and to visit the frost-bitten shores of northeastern Siberia and northwestern Alaska. So enticing was the lure of this new adventure, so eager was he to study the evidence of glaciation in the Far North, that he said a reluctant good-bye to his young wife and fared forth upon the deep. "You remember," he wrote to her from the Siberian coast, "that I told you long ago how eager I was to get upon those islands in the middle of the Bering Sea and Strait to read the ice record there."

The events which led up to this memorable cruise of the Corwin in 1881 had their origin in the widespread interest which north polar exploration was exciting at this time all over the world. In 1877 Lieutenant George W. De Long, an American naval officer, was searching among the northern ports of England for a whaling vessel adapted to the requirements of Arctic exploration. De Long had commanded the Juniata which was sent out for the relief of the Polaris, and through this experience had grown enthusiastic over his own plans for reaching the North Pole.

The whaling industry was at that time a very profitable one, and few owners of whalers and sealers were willing to part with their vessels. Though Sir Allen Young's steam yacht Pandora, which De Long finally selected, had already made two Arctic voyages, she appears to have been chosen more because she was available than because of her superior fitness for ice navigation. In any case she was purchased by James Gordon Bennett, patron of the proposed expedition, was fitted out at Deptford, England, and renamed the Jeannette. Though the new name evaded the suggestion of a box of evils, she proved to be one for those who sailed in her. Commander De Long himself brought her around Cape Horn to San Francisco. In the month of July, 1879, she sailed from that port for Bering Strait and the Arctic Ocean—never to return. Crushed in the ice, she sank, June 12, 1881, in the Arctic Ocean, one hundred and fifty miles north of the New Siberian Islands.

The retreat southward across the ice-floes was one of great peril. Only thirteen out of thirty-four men ultimately reached civilization and safety. De Long himself, and ten of the men with him, died of starvation and exposure on the delta of the Lena River, where two of the Jeannette's storm-beaten cutters landed in the middle of September, 1881. One of them, commanded by Chief Engineer Melville, reached a Russian village on one of the eastern mouths of the Lena River. He promptly organized a search party, recovering the ship's records in November, 1881, and the bodies of his unfortunate shipmates the following spring.

When the North Pacific whaling fleet returned from Arctic waters in the autumn of 1879, two ships, the Mount Wollaston and the Vigilant, were reported missing. They had been last seen in October in the same general region, near Herald Island, where the Jeannette had entered the polar ice. The Mount Wollaston was commanded by Captain Nye, of New Bedford, Massachusetts, one of the keenest and bravest men that ever sailed the frigid seas. He it

Introduction

was who at a conference of whaling captains, called by De Long in San Francisco before the departure of his expedition, hesitated to give an opinion on the practicability of De Long's plans. But when urged for an expression of his views, he said, "Put her [the Jeannette] into the ice and let her drift, and you may get through, or you may go to the devil, and the chances are about equal."

In the service of the United States Treasury Department there was at this time a staunch little steamer called the Corwin. Built at Abina, Oregon, she was constructed throughout of the finest Oregon fir, fastened with copper, galvanized iron, and locust-tree nails. She had a draught of nearly eleven feet, twenty-four feet beam, and was one hundred and thirty-seven feet long between perpendiculars. The ordinary duties of the captain of such a revenue steamer involved primarily the enforcement of federal laws for the protection of governmental interests on the Fur Seal Islands and the sea-otter hunting grounds of Alaska. But the supposed plight of the Jeannette and the unknown fate of two whalers caught in the ice were soon to increase the Corwin's duties, and call her into regions where her sturdy sailing qualities were to prove of the utmost importance.

In the spring of 1880 the Corwin, in command of Captain Calvin L. Hooper, was ordered into North Alaskan waters in pursuance of her regular duties. But Captain Hooper had also been directed to make all possible inquiries for the missing whalers and the Jeannette. He returned with no tidings of the lost, but with reports of starvation and death among the Eskimos of St. Lawrence Island on account of an uncommonly severe and stormy winter in the Arctic regions. He entertained no hope for the lost whalers, but thought De Long and his party might be safe.

A general demand for relief expeditions now arose. Petitions

Introduction

poured into Congress, and the American Geographical Society addressed a forcible appeal to President Garfield. When the Corwin was sent to Alaskan waters again in 1881 it was with the following specific instructions to Captain Hooper:

> No information having been received concerning the whalers Mount Wollaston and Vigilant, you will bear in mind the instructions for your cruise of last year, and it is hoped you may bring back some tidings of the missing vessels. You will also make careful inquiries in the Arctic regarding the progress and whereabouts of the steamer Jeannette, engaged in making explorations under command of Lieutenant-Commander De Long, U.S.N., and will, if practicable, communicate with and extend any needed assistance to that vessel. . . . You will in your season's cruise touch at such places as may be practicable on the mainland or islands where there are settlements of natives, and examine into and report upon their condition.

A letter written to his mother from Dutch Harbor, Unalaska, gives Muir's own account of his purpose in joining the expedition.

> I wrote you from San Francisco [he says] that I had suddenly made up my mind to avail myself of the opportunity offered to visit the Arctic region on the steamer Thomas Corwin sent to seek the Jeannette and the missing whalers that were lost in the ice two years ago off Point Barrow. . . .
> I have been interested for a long time in the glaciation of the Pacific Coast, and I felt that I must make a trip of this sort to the Far North some time, and no better chance could in any

probability offer. I am acquainted with our captain, and have every comfort the ship can afford, and every facility to pursue my studies.

We mean to proceed from here past the seal islands St. Paul and St. George, then northward along the Siberian coast to about Cape Serdze, where a sledge party with dogs will be sent out to search the North Siberian coast, while the steamer the meanwhile will cross to the American shore and call at St. Michael, Kotzebue Sound, and other places, [where we shall have the opportunity of] making short journeys inland. Then, as the ice melts and breaks up, we will probably push eastward around Point Barrow, then return to the Siberian side to pick up our land party, then endeavor to push through the ice to the mysterious unexplored Wrangell Land. We hope to return to San Francisco by October or November, but may possibly be compelled to winter in the Arctic somewhere.

De Long, in a letter to his wife, had written that his plan was to *proceed north by the eastern coast of Wrangell Land,* touching first at Herald Island to build a cairn and leave news of the Jeannette's progress. Believing that Wrangell Land extended northward toward the Pole, he proposed to leave similar records along its eastern coast, under cairns, at intervals of twenty-five miles. These known intentions of De Long show why it was one of the foremost objects of the Corwin expedition to reach what Muir called "the mysterious unexplored Wrangell Land."

How keenly Muir appreciated the possibilities of science and adventure in the exploration of this unknown Arctic land may be seen in the fourteenth chapter of this volume. Up to this time

Introduction

nothing was actually known about Wrangell Land except its existence. The first European who reported its discovery was Captain Kellett of H.M.S. Herald. He saw it in 1849 when he discovered Herald Island, which was named after his vessel. By right of discovery Kellett's name should have been given to Wrangell Land, and upon British Admiralty charts it was very properly indicated as "Kellett Land."

The name Wrangell Land, it seems, became associated with the island through a report of Captain Thomas Long, of the whaling bark Nile. In 1867 he reported that he had

> sailed to the eastward along the land during the fifteenth and part of the sixteenth [of August], and in some places approached it as near as fifteen miles. I have named this northern land Wrangell Land [he says] as an appropriate tribute to the memory of a man who spent three consecutive years north of latitude 68°, and demonstrated the problem of this open polar sea forty-five years ago, although others of much later date have endeavored to claim the merit of this discovery. The west cape of this land I have named Cape Thomas, after the man who first reported the land from the masthead of my ship, and the southeastern cape I have named after the largest island in this group [Hawaii].[1]

Captain Long apparently was unaware of the fact that the island already bore the name of Kellett by right of discovery eighteen years earlier. But since Baron Wrangell had made such a brave and

[1]Quoted from a letter by Captain Long published in the *Honolulu Commercial Advertiser*, November, 1867. The same paper contains a letter from Captain George W. Raynor, of the ship Reindeer, giving additional geographic details.

Introduction

determined search for this "problematical land of the North," as he referred to it in his final report, there is a certain poetic justice in applying his name to what he only sought, but never found.

While Captain Hooper, in his report of 1880, had expressed the conviction that Wrangell Land was an island, the first demonstration of its insularity was made by Commander De Long, who had practically staked the success of his expedition on the belief that it was a country of large extent northward, and suitable for winter quarters. But before his vessel was crushed in the ice it drifted, within sight of Wrangell Land, directly across the meridians between which it lies. This fatal drift of the Jeannette not only furnished conclusive disproof of the theory that Wrangell Land might be part of a continent stretching across the north polar regions, but proved it to be an island of limited extent. It is an inaccuracy, therefore, when the United States Hydrographer's report for 1882 sets the establishment of this fact down to the credit of the Rodgers expedition.

So far as known, the first human beings that ever stood upon the shores of this island were in Captain Hooper's landing party, August 12, 1881, and John Muir was of the number. The earliest news of the event, and of the fact that De Long had not succeeded in touching either Herald Island or Wrangell Land, reached the world at large in a letter from Muir published in the *San Francisco Evening Bulletin*, September 29, 1881. But the complete record of Muir's observations, together with some of the sketches contained in his journals, is now given to the public for the first time.

A second Jeannette relief expedition, already mentioned as that of the Rodgers, was sent out under the direction of the Secretary of the Navy. It succeeded in reaching Wrangell Land two weeks after the Corwin. In order to make our geographical and scientific knowledge of this remote island as complete in this volume as possible, we deem it desirable to include a brief account of what was achieved during the cruise of the Rodgers.

This vessel, a stout and comparatively new whaler, known before its re-baptism as the Mary and Helen, was placed in command of Lieutenant, now Rear Admiral, Robert M. Berry. He discovered on the southern shore of Wrangell Land a snug little harbor where he kept the Rodgers at anchor for nineteen days while two search parties, in whaleboats, going in opposite directions, explored the coast for possible survivors of the missing whalers and for cairns left by the crew of the Jeannette. These search parties nearly circumnavigated the island without finding anything except Captain Hooper's cairn, and Commander Berry, in his report to the Secretary of the Navy, said, "I believe it impossible that any of the missing parties ever landed here."

The principal gain of this exploration was a running survey of the coast and a general determination of the size of the island. In other respects the harvest of scientific facts gathered on Wrangell Land by the Rodgers was meager, if one may judge by W. H. Gilder's *Ice Pack and Tundra*. Unfortunately, the act which carried the appropriation for the expedition provided that the vessel selected "be wholly manned by volunteers from the Navy." This fact seems to have prevented the taking of men trained in the natural sciences, like John Muir or E. W. Nelson. Nineteen days on Wrangell Land would have enabled them to obtain a large amount of interesting information about its flora, fauna, avifauna, and geology.

Commander Berry, taking charge of an exploring party, penetrated twenty miles into the interior of the island and ascended a conspicuous mountain whose height, by barometric measurement, was found to be twenty-five hundred feet. He reported that he "could see from its summit the sea in all directions, except between S.S.W. by W. per compass. The day was very clear, and no land except Herald Island was visible from this height. There was no ice in sight to the southward." A letter of inquiry addressed to Rear Admiral Berry by the editor brought a courteous reply, stating that he did not know of any photographs or sketches, made by members of the Rodgers expedition, which would show the coast or interior topography of the island; that "the vegetation was scant, consisting of a few Arctic plants, a little moss, etc."; that "polar bears, walrus, and seal were quite common upon or near the island," and that the provisional map which accompanied his report to the Secretary of the Navy in 1881 is the only one available.

From our reproduction of this map, and from the report of the Rodgers, it will be seen that practically the whole interior of the island still awaits exploration. Estimates of its size vary between twenty-eight and forty miles as to width, and between sixty-five and seventy-five as to length. Striking an average, one might say that it contains about twenty-five hundred square miles of territory. The distance across Long Strait from the nearest point on the Siberian coast is about eighty-five or ninety miles, and Herald Island lies about thirty miles east of Wrangell Land.

In 1914 the Karluk, Steffánsson's flagship of the Canadian Arctic Expedition, was crushed in the ice, and sank not far from the place where the Jeannette was lost. Under the able leadership of Captain Robert A. Bartlett the members of the expedition made their way to Wrangell Land, where they remained encamped while Captain Bartlett, with an Eskimo, crossed Long's Strait to Siberia

Introduction

over the ice. Thence he made his way to St. Michael, Alaska, and enlisted aid for the Karluk survivors. Their rescue was effected successfully, and, so far as we are able to discover, these members of the Canadian Arctic Expedition are the only human beings that have been on Wrangell Land since the visit of the Corwin and the Rodgers in 1881.

We venture to mention, in this connection, a few facts which call for consideration in the interest of a historical and consistent geographical nomenclature. The United States Geographic Board has done much to bring order out of the chaos of Alaskan names, and its decisions are available in Baker's *Geographic Dictionary of Alaska*, which has been followed in the editing of this volume. There is a "Wrangell Island" in southeastern Alaska, well known to readers of Muir's *Travels in Alaska*, hence it occasions needless confusion to call Wrangell Land by the same name, as even recent Hydrographic Office charts continue to do, besides misspelling the name. The retention of the term "land" for an island is supported by abundant precedent, especially in the Arctic regions.

The altitude of the mountain ascended by Commander Berry had already been determined with remarkable accuracy by Captain Long in 1867. He described it as having "the appearance of an extinct volcano," and it is shown on his sketch of Wrangell Land, reproduced on the map accompanying Nourse's *American Explorations in the Ice Zones*. Captain Hooper, in his report of the cruise of the Corwin, declares that the peak had been appropriately named for Long, and adds, "Singular as it may appear, this name to which Captain Long was justly entitled has, notwithstanding our pretended custom of adhering to original names, been set aside on a recent issue of American charts." It is some compensation,

Introduction

however, that the wide stretch of water between the North Siberian coast and Wrangell Land is now known as Long Strait.

Captain Hooper and his party, being the first to set foot upon Wrangell Land, exercised the privilege of taking possession of it in the name of the United States. In order to avoid the confusion of the two names, Kellett and Wrangell, which it already bore, Captain Hooper named it New Columbia. This name, which was set aside by the Hydrographic Office, he says

was suggested by the name which had been given to the islands farther west, New Siberia. It is probable that the name Wrangell Land will continue in use upon American charts, but its justice, in view of all the facts, is not so apparent. In my opinion the adoption by us of the name Kellett Land given by the English would be appropriate, and avoid the confusion which is sure to follow in consequence of its having two names.

Headlands and other geographical features of the island were named by us, but as the names which were applied to features actually discovered by the Corwin and heretofore unnamed have been ignored, it is possible that a desire to do honor to the memory of Wrangell is not the only consideration. To avoid the complications which would result from duplicating geographical names, I have dropped all bestowed by the Corwin and adopted *the more recent ones* applied by the Hydrographic Office. I have also adopted the plan of the island [from surveys of the Rodgers] as shown on the small chart accompanying Hydrographic Notice No. 84, although the trend of the coast and the geographical position of the mouth of the river where we

Introduction

first planted the flag do not agree with the result of the observations and triangulations made by the Corwin.

Now that Captain Hooper and nearly all the men who had a share in these explorations of the early eighties have passed on, it is proper that the basic facts as well as conflicting judgments should be set down here for the just consideration of geographers. Both from Muir's vivid narrative of the Corwin's penetration to the shores of Wrangell Land, and from Captain Hooper's admirable report published in 1884 as Senate Executive Document No. 204, the reader will conclude that the Captain of the Corwin had a better right to be remembered in connection with the geographical features of the island than most of the persons whose names have been attached to them by the Hydrographic Office.

Whether Wrangell Land became United States territory when Hooper formally raised our flag over it is a question. The editor is unable to discover any treaty between Russia and the United States which would debar possession by the latter. But questions involving rights of territorial discovery have not, so far as we know, been raised between the two governments.

Muir's opportunity to join the Corwin apparently arose out of his acquaintanceship with Captain Hooper, and when the invitation came he had little time to prepare for the cruise. A letter to his wife affords a glimpse of his surroundings and plans when the Corwin was approaching Unalaska:

All goes well on our little ship [he writes] and not all the tossing of the waves, and the snow and hail on the deck, and being out of sight of land so long, can make me surely feel that

Introduction

I am not now with you all as ever, so sudden was my departure, and so long have I been accustomed in the old lonely life to feel the influence of loved ones as if present in the flesh, while yet far. . . . There are but three of us in the cabin, the Captain, the Surgeon, and myself, and only the same three at table, so that there is no crowding. . . .

Should we be successful in reaching Wrangell Land we would very likely be compelled to winter on it, exploring while the weather permitted. In case we are unsuccessful in reaching Wrangell Land, we may get caught farther west and be able to reach it by dog-sledges in winter while the pack is frozen. Or we may have to winter on the Siberian coast, etc., etc., according to the many variable known and unknown circumstances of the case. Of course if De Long is found we will return at once. If not, a persistent effort will be made to force a way to that mysterious ice-girt Wrangell Land, since it was to it that De Long was directing his efforts when last heard from. We will be cautious, however, and we hope to be back to our homes this fall. Do not allow this outline of Captain Hooper's plan to get into print at present.

From another letter written the following day we quote this breezy bit of description:—

How cold it is this morning! How it blows and snows! It is not "the wolf's long howl on Unalaska's shore," as Campbell has it, but the wind's long howl. A more sustained, prolonged, screeching, raving howl I never before heard. But the little Corwin rides on through it in calm strength, rising and falling amid

Introduction

the foam-streaked waves like a loon. The cabin boy, Henry, told me this morning [May 16] early that land was in sight. So I got up at six o'clock—nine of your time—and went up into the pilot-house to see it. Two jagged black masses were visible, with hints of snow mountains back of them, but mostly hidden beneath a snow-storm.

After breakfast we were within two miles of the shore. Huge snow-peaks, grandly ice-sculptured, loomed far into the stormy sky for a few moments in tolerably clear relief; then the onrush of snowflakes, sweeping out into the dark levels of the sea, would hide it all and fill our eyes, while we puckered our brows and tried to gaze into the face of it all.

We have to proceed in the dimness and confusion of the storm with great caution, stopping frequently to take soundings, so it will probably be one or two o'clock before we reach the harbor of Unalaska on the other side of the island. I tried an hour ago to make a sketch of the mountains along the shore for you, to be sent with this letter, but my fingers got too cold to hold the pencil, and the snow filled my eyes, and so dimmed the outlines of the rocks that I could not trace them.

Down here in the cabin it is warm and summerish, and when the Captain and Doctor are on deck I have it all to myself. . . . I am glad you thought to send my glasses and barometer and coat. We will procure furs as we proceed north, so as to be ready in case we should be compelled to winter in the Arctic regions. It is remarkably cold even here, and dark and blue and forbidding every way, though it is fine weather for health.

I was just thinking this morning of our warm sunny home . . . and of the red cherries down the hill, and the hundreds of

Introduction

blunt-billed finches, every one of them with red bills soaked in cherry juice. Not much fruit juice beneath this sky!

During the cruise Muir kept a daily record of his experiences and observations. He also wrote a series of letters to the *San Francisco Evening Bulletin* in which he turned to account the contents of his journal. Comparison of the letters with the journal shows that his note-books contain a large amount of interesting literary and scientific material which has not been utilized in the *Bulletin* letters. To publish both would involve too much duplication. It has seemed best, therefore, to make the letters the foundation of the volume and to insert the additional matter from the journal wherever it belongs chronologically in the epistolary record. Most of the letters have thus grown far beyond their original size.

The performance of this task has often been trying and time-consuming, especially when it became the editor's duty to avoid repetition, or overlapping, by selecting what seemed to be the more comprehensive, the more finished, or the more vivid form of statement. But this method of solving the difficulty has the advantage, for the reader, of unifying in the present volume practically the whole of Muir's literary and scientific work during the cruise of the Corwin. Sometimes, as in chapters eleven and twelve, all the material is new and has been derived exclusively from the journal. The style of the latter may generally be recognized by its telegraphic conciseness.

During his studies in the Sierra Nevada Muir had acquired skill, speed, and accuracy in sketching the features of a landscape. This ability he turned to good account during the cruise of the Corwin, for one of his journals is filled with a variety of sketches which prove to be remarkably faithful pictures in cases where it has been possible to compare them with photographs.

Since Muir's primary object in joining the Corwin expedition was to look for evidence of glaciation in the Arctic and subarctic regions, we have deemed it desirable to include in this volume the article in which he gathered up the results of his glacial studies and discoveries. It was published in 1884, with Captain C. L. Hooper's report, as Senate Executive Document No. 204 of the Forty-eighth Congress.

Both the Hooper report and the article on glaciation were elaborately illustrated from Muir's pencil sketches, though the fact that they were Muir's is nowhere stated. "The 'Glacier Article' arrived on the sixth," wrote Captain Hooper to Muir under date of February 7, 1884, "and was sent on its way rejoicing the same day. The Honorable Secretary [of the Treasury] assures me that he will see that the whole is printed without delay. Please accept my thanks for the article, which is very interesting. The sketches are very fine and will prove a valuable addition to the report. That of the large glacier from Mount Fairweather is particularly fine."

The article on glaciation should have been published a year earlier, in the same volume with the "Botanical Notes." But for some reason Muir was misinformed, and an apologetic letter to him from Major E. W. Clark, then Chief of the United States Revenue Marine, hints at a petty intrigue as the cause. "I regret very much," he writes, "that I had not myself corresponded with you regarding your contribution to the Arctic report. Your article on glaciation would have been exactly the thing and would have admitted of very effective illustration. I feel well assured that you were purposely misinformed regarding the report, and could readily ex-

Introduction

plain the reason to you in a personal interview. There has been
much anxious inquiry for your notes on glaciation." It was the
writer of this letter after whom Captain Hooper named the river at
whose mouth the Corwin anchored on Wrangell Land. This fact
has been recorded by Professor Joseph Everett Nourse, U.S.N., in
his work *American Explorations in the Ice Zones*. He states that
through the courtesy of Major Clark he had access to the unpublished official report of the cruise of the Corwin. Since the river in
question appears without a name upon the chart of Wrangell
Land, we must suppose it to be one of the names which Captain
Hooper complains the Hydrographic Office ignored.

Besides the illustrative drawings which accompany Muir's
article on glaciation in the Far North, his note-books contain
numerous interesting sketches of geological and topographical features of Arctic landscapes. They show with what tireless industry
and pains he worked at his task. This is the first publication of the
general conclusions of his Arctic studies, supported in detail by the
records of his journal. In its present form the article follows a re-
vised copy found among Muir's papers.

Muir's report on the flora of Herald Island and Wrangell Land
still remains, after thirty-six years, the only one ever made on the
vegetation of these remote Arctic regions. It has seemed best,
therefore, to include also his article entitled "Botanical Notes" as
an appendix to this volume. It was first published in 1883 as a part
of Treasury Department Document No. 429. Strangely enough,
the letter of transmittal from the Secretary of the Treasury refers to
it as "the observations on glaciation in the Arctic Ocean and the
Alaska region made by John Muir."

The author never saw printer's proof after he sent the manu-

[xxvii]

Introduction

script, and the number of typographical errors made in the technical parts of his article must have established a new record, for they mount into hundreds. Knowing that Muir had sent a duplicate set of his Arctic plant collection to Dr. Asa Gray for final scientific determination, the editor went to the Gray Herbarium of Harvard University, in order to make the necessary corrections and verifications. Fortunately the writer found there not only the original plants, but also Muir's letters to Asa Gray. "I returned a week ago," wrote Muir under date of October 31, 1881, "from the polar region around Wrangell Land and Herald Island, and brought a few plants from there which I wish you would name as soon as convenient, as I have to write a report on the flora for the expedition. I had a fine icy time, and gathered a lot of exceedingly interesting facts concerning the formation of Bering Sea and the Arctic Ocean, and the configuration of the shores of Siberia and Alaska. Also concerning the forests that used to grow there, etc., which I hope some day to discuss with you."

The editor has made no attempt to reduce the genus and species names to modern synonymy. As in the case of Muir's *A Thousand-Mile Walk to the Gulf*, it has seemed best to offer the original determinations, making the necessary corrections by reference to the *Index Kewensis*, and, in the case of the ferns, to Christensen's *Index Filicum*. Since Muir's lists did not follow any particular order of classification we have adopted the order of families laid down in the last edition of Gray's *Manual of Botany*.

Special interest attaches to the fact that Muir found on the Arctic shore of Alaska, near Cape Thompson, a species of *Erigeron* new to science. It is an asteraceous plant with showy, daisy-like flowers. In reporting this find to the American Academy of Arts

Introduction

and Sciences, Asa Gray described it as "the most interesting and apparently the only new species of an extensive and truly valuable collection made by Mr. Muir in a recent searching cruise which he accompanied, and which extended to Wrangel Island [Wrangell Land]. The plant seems to have been abundant, for it occurs in the collection under three numbers."

Gray promptly named it *Erigeron Muirii* in honor of its finder, thus redeeming for the second time a promise made ten years earlier when he wrote to Muir, "Pray, find a new genus, or at least a new species, that I may have the satisfaction of embalming your name, not in glacier ice, but in spicy wild perfume."

William Frederic Badè
1917

1

Unalaska and the Aleuts

UNALASKA, MAY 18, 1881   The Storm King of the North is abroad to-day, working with a fine, hearty enthusiasm, rolling a multitude of white combing waves through the rocky, jagged straits between this marvelous chain of islands, circling them about with beaten foam, and heaping a lavish abundance of snow on their lofty, cloud-wrapped mountains. The deep bass of the gale, sounding on through the rugged, ice-sculptured peaks and gorges, is delightful music to our ears, now that we are safely sheltered in a land-locked harbor.

The steamer Thomas Corwin arrived here about noon to-day, after a prosperous run of thirteen days from San Francisco, intending to take on coal and additional supplies of every kind for her long cruise in the Arctic in search of the Jeannette and the missing whalers. Nothing especially noteworthy occurred on the voyage. The weather was remarkably cold for this season of the year, the average temperature for the first day or two being about 55° F., falling gradually to 35° as we approached Unalaska, accompanied by blustering squalls of snow and hail, suggestive of much higher latitudes than this.

On the morning of the fifteenth we met a gale from the northeast, against which the Corwin forced her way with easy strength,

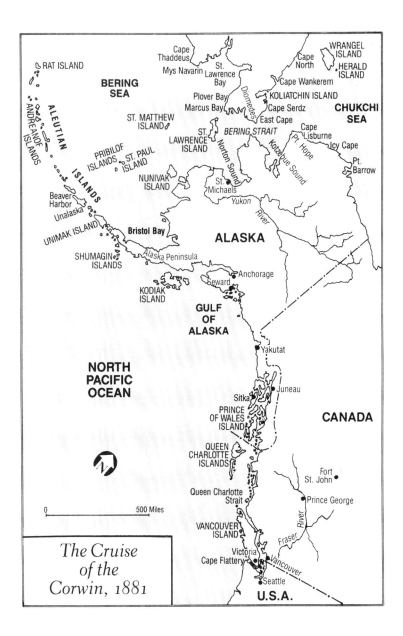

RAT ISLAND

ALEUTIAN ANDREANOF ISLANDS

BERING
SEA

Cape
Thaddeus
Mys Navarin St.
Lawrence
Bay
Plover Bay
Marcus Bay

ST. MATTHEW
ISLAND

ST.
LAWRENCE
ISLAND

Diomedes

BERING STRAIT

East Cape

Cape
North

WRANGEL
ISLAND

HERALD
ISLAND

Cape Wankerem

KOLIATCHIN ISLAND

Cape Serdz

CHUKCHI
SEA

Cape
Lisburne

Pt. Hope

Icy Cape

Pt.
Barrow

ISLANDS

PRIBILOF
ISLANDS ST. PAUL
ISLAND

NUNIVAK
ISLAND

Norton Sound

St.
Michaels

Kotzebue Sound

Beaver
Harbor

Unalaska

UNIMAK ISLAND

Bristol Bay

Alaska Peninsula

Yukon   River

ALASKA

SHUMAGIN
ISLANDS

KODIAK
ISLAND

Seward

Anchorage

GULF
OF
ALASKA

Yakutat

NORTH
PACIFIC
OCEAN

Sitka

PRINCE
OF WALES
ISLAND

Juneau

CANADA

QUEEN
CHARLOTTE
ISLANDS

Fort
St. John

Queen Charlotte
Strait

Prince George

0   500 Miles

VANCOUVER
ISLAND

Fraser

River

The Cruise
of the
Corwin, 1881

Victoria
Cape Flattery

Vancouver

Seattle

U.S.A.

rising and falling on the foam-streaked waves as lightly as a duck. We first sighted land on the morning of the seventeenth, near the southeast extremity of Unalaska Island. Two black outstanding masses of jagged lava were visible, with the bases of snowy peaks back of them, while all the highlands were buried beneath storm-clouds. After we had approached within three or four miles of the shore, a ragged opening in the clouds disclosed a closely packed cluster of peaks, laden with snow, looming far into the stormy sky for a few moments in tolerably clear relief, then fading again in the gloom of the clouds and fresh squalls of blinding snow and hail. The fall of the snowflakes among the dark, heaving waves and curling breakers was a most impressive sight.

Groping cautiously along the coast, we at length entered the Akutan Pass. A heavy flood tide was setting through it against the northeast gale, which raised a heavy sea. The waves reared as if about to fall backward, while the wind tore off their white curling tops and carried them away in the form of gray scud. Never before have I seen the sea in so hearty and exhilarating a motion. It was all one white, howling, rampant, runaway mass of foam from side to side. We feared getting our decks swept. Caught, therefore, as we were between the tide and the gale, we turned to seek shelter and wait better times.

We found good anchorage in the lee of a red lava bluff near Cook's Harbor, a few miles to the westward of the mouth of the Pass. The sailors got out their cod-lines, and in a few minutes a dozen fine cod were flapping on the deck. They proved to be excellent fish, eaten fresh. But whether they are as good as the renowned Newfoundland article I cannot judge, as I never have tasted fresh cod. The storm sounding on over the mountains made fine music while we lay safely at anchor, and we enjoyed it all the more because we were in a wild, nameless place that we had ourselves discovered.

The next morning, the gale having abated somewhat, we entered the strait. Wind and tide were flowing in company, but they were against us, and so strong was the latter that we could not stem it, and were compelled to fall back until it was near the turn. The Aleutian chain extends across from continent to continent like an imperfect dam between the Pacific and Bering Sea, and through the gaps between the islands the tide rushes with tremendous speed and uproar. When the tide was favorable, we weighed anchor and passed through the strait and around Kalekta Point into this magnificent harbor[1] without further difficulty.

The harbor of Unalaska is excellent, land-locked, and has a good holding bottom. By virtue of its geographical position it is likely to remain for a long time the business center of western Alaska. The town [2] is situated on a washed and outspread terminal moraine at the mouth of one of the main glaciers that united here to excavate the harbor. Just above the village there is a glacial lake only a few feet above tide, and a considerable area of level ground about it where the cattle belonging to the town find abundance of fine grass.

Early in the forenoon the clouds had lifted and the sun had

[1]Dutch Harbor, on the eastern side of Amaknck Island in Unalaska Bay.
[2]The chief town of Unalaska Island, the most important of the eastern Aleutians, is Iliuliuk. It was founded by Solovief during the decade between 1760 and 1770, and its Aleut name, according to one interpretation, means "harmony," according to another, "the curved beach." The name Unalaska is often applied loosely to the town as well as the island.

come out, revealing a host of noble mountains, grandly sculptured and composed, and robed in spotless white, some of the highest adorned with streamers of mealy snow wavering in the wind—a truly glorious spectacle. To me the features of greatest interest in this imposing show were the glacial advertisements everywhere displayed in clear, telling characters—the trends of the numerous inlets and cañons pointing back into the ancient ice-fountains among the peaks, the sculpture of the peaks themselves and their general outlines, and the shorn faces of the cliffs fronting the sea. No clearer and more unmistakable glacial inscriptions are to be found upon any portion of the mountain ranges of the Pacific Coast.

It seems to be guessed in a general way by most observers who have made brief visits to this region that all the islands of the Aleutian chain are clearly volcanic upheavals, scarce at all changed since the period of their emergence from the sea. This is an impression made, no doubt, by the volcanic character of the rocks of which they are composed, and by the numerous extinct and active volcanoes occurring here and there along the summits of the highest masses. But it is plain that the amount of glacial denudation which these ancient lavas have undergone is very great; so great that now every feature presented, with the exception of the few recent craters, is glacial.

The glaciers, that a short time ago covered all the islands, have sculptured the comparatively featureless rock masses into separate mountain peaks, and perhaps into separate islands. Certainly they have done this in some cases. All the inlets or fiords, also, that I have seen are simply the channels of the larger of those old ice rivers that flowed into the sea and eroded their beds beneath its level. The size and the trend of every one of these fiords correspond invariably with the size and the trend of the glacier basin at its head, while not a single fiord or cañon may be found that does not conduct back to mountain fountains whence the eroding glacier drew its sources. The Alaska Peninsula, before the coming on of the glacial period, may have comprehended the whole of the Aleutian chain, its present condition being mostly due to the down-grinding action of ice. Frost and fire have worked hand in hand to produce the grand effects presented in this majestic crescent of islands.

UNALASKA, MAY 21, 1881   The Aleutian chain of islands is one of the most remarkable and interesting to be found on the globe. It sweeps in a regular curve a thousand miles long from the end of the Alaska Peninsula towards Kamchatka and nearly unites the American and Asiatic continents. A very short geological time ago, just before the coming on of the glacial period, this connection of the continents was probably complete, inasmuch as the entire chain is simply a degraded portion of the North American coast mountains, with its foothills and connecting ridges between the summit peaks a few feet under water. These submerged ridges form the passes between the islands as they exist to-day, while it is evident that this segregating degradation has been effected by the majestic down-grinding glaciers that lately loaded all the chain. Only a few wasting remnants of these glaciers are now in existence, lingering in the highest, snowiest fountains on the largest of the islands.

The mountains are from three thousand to nine thousand feet high, many of them capped with perpetual snow, and rendered yet more imposing by volcanoes emitting smoke and ashes—the feeble manifestations of upbuilding volcanic force that was active long before the beginning of the great ice winter. To the traveler from the south, approaching any portion of the chain during the winter or spring months, the view presented is exceedingly desolate and forbidding. The snow comes down to the water's edge, the solid winter-white being interrupted only by black outstanding bluffs with faces too sheer for snow to lie upon, and by the backs of clustering rocks and long rugged reefs beaten and overswept by heavy breakers rolling in from the Pacific Ocean or Bering Sea, while for ten or eleven months in the year all the mountains are wrapped in gloomy, ragged storm-clouds.

Nevertheless, there is no lack of warm, eager life even here. The stormy shores swarm with fishes—cod, halibut, herring, salmon trout, etc.; also with whales, seals, and many species of water birds, while the sea-otter, the most valuable of the fur-bearing animals, finds its favorite home about the outlying wave-washed reefs. The only land animals occurring in considerable numbers are, as far as I have been able to learn, three or four species of foxes, which are distributed from one end of the chain to the other, with the Arctic grouse, the raven, snowbirds, wrens, and a few finches. There are no deer, wild sheep, goats, bears, or wolves, though all of these are abundant on the mainland in the same latitude.

In two short excursions that I made to the top of a mountain, about two thousand feet high, back of the settlement here, and to a grassy island in the harbor, I found the snow in some places well tracked by foxes and grouse, and saw six species of birds, mostly solitary or in twos and threes. The vegetation near the level of the sea and on bare windswept ridges, up to a height of a thousand feet or more, is remarkably close and luxuriant, covering every foot of the ground.

First there is a dense plush of mosses and lichens from six inches to a foot in depth. Out of the moss mantle and over it there grow five or six species of good nutritious grasses, the tallest shoulder-high; also three species of vaccinium, cranberry, empetrum, the delightful linnæa in extensive patches, the beautiful purple-flowered bryanthus, a pyrola, two species of dwarf willow, three of lycopodium, two saxifrages, a lupine, wild pea, archangelica, geranium, anemone, draba, bearberry, and the little goldthread coptis, besides two ferns and a few withered specimens that I could not make out.

The anemone, draba, and bearberry are already in bloom; the willows are beginning to show the ends of their silky catkins, and a good many green leaves are springing up in sheltered places near the level of the sea. At a height of four or five hundred feet, however, winter still holds sway, with scarce a memory of the rich and beautiful bloom of the summer time. How beautiful these mountains must be when all are in bloom, with the bland summer sunshine on them, the butterflies and bees among them, and the deep glacial fiords calm and full of reflections! The tall grasses, with their showy purple panicles in flower, waving in the wind over all the lower mountain slopes, with a growth heavy enough for the scythe, must then be a beautiful sight, and so must the broad patches of heathworts with their multitude of pink bells, and the tall lupines and ferns along the banks of the streams.

There is not a tree of any kind on the islands excepting a few spruces brought from Sitka and planted by the Russians some fifty years ago. They are still alive, but have made very little growth—a circumstance no doubt due to the climate. But in what respect it differs from the climate of southeastern Alaska, lying both north and south of this latitude, where forests flourish exuberantly in all kinds of exposures, on rich alluvium or on bare rocks, I am unable to say. The only wood I noticed, and all that is said to exist on any of the islands, is small patches of willow, with stems an inch thick, and of several species of woody-stemmed heathworts; this the native Aleuts gather for fuel, together with small quantities of driftwood cast on the shores by the winds and currents.

Grass of good quality for stock is abundant on all the larger islands, and cattle thrive and grow fat during the summer wherever they have been tried. But the wetness of the summer months will always prevent hay from being made in any considerable quantity and make stock-raising on anything like a large scale impossible.

The agricultural possibilities of the islands are also very limited. Oats and barley head out but never fully mature, and if they did, it would be very difficult to get them dry enough for the granary. Potatoes, lettuce, cabbage, turnips, beets, etc., do well in spots that are well drained and have a southern exposure.

According to the census taken last year, the inhabitants of these islands number 2451. Of this population 82 are whites, 479 creoles, and 1890 Aleuts. The Aleuts are far more civilized and Christianized than any other tribe of Alaska Indians. From a third to one half of the men and women read and write. Their occupation is the hunting of the sea-otter for the Alaska Commercial Company.

A good hunter makes from four hundred to eight hundred dollars per annum. In this pursuit they go hundreds of miles in their frail skin-covered canoes, which are so light that they may easily be carried under one's arm. Earning so much money, they are able to support themselves with many comforts beyond the reach of most of the laboring classes of Europe. Nevertheless, with all their advantages, they are fading away like other Indians. The deaths exceed the births in nearly every one of their villages, and it is only a question of time when they will vanish from the face of the earth.

On the way back to the ship I sauntered through the town. It contains about one hundred buildings, half of them frame, built by the Alaska Commercial and Western Fur and Trading Companies. Aleutian huts are called "barábaras." They are built of turf on a frame of wood; some of them have floors, and are divided into many rooms, very small ones. The smells are horrible to clean nostrils, and the air is foul and dead beyond endurance. Some of the bedrooms are not much larger than coffins. The floors are below the surface of the ground two or three feet, and the doors are at the end away from the direction of the prevailing wind. There are one or two small windows of glass or bladder, and a small pipe surmounts a very small Russian stove in which the stems of empetrum are burned.

In most of the huts that I entered I found a Yankee clock, a few pictures, and ordinary cheap crockery and furniture; accordions, also, as they are fond of music. All such bits of furniture and finery of foreign manufacture contrast meanly with their old-fashioned kind. Altogether, in dress and home gear, they are so meanly mixed, savage and civilized, that they make a most pathetic impression. The moisture rained down upon them every other day keeps the walls and the roof green, even flowery, and as perfectly fresh as the sod before it was built into a hut. Goats, once intro-

Unalaska and the Aleuts

duced by the Russians, make these hut tops their favorite play and pasture grounds, much to the annoyance of their occupants. In one of these huts I saw for the first time arrowheads manufactured out of bottle glass. The edges are chipped by hard pressure with a bit of deer horn.

As the Tlingit Indians of the Alexander Archipelago make their own whiskey, so these Aleuts make their own beer, an intoxicating drink, which, if possible, is more abominable and destructive than hootchenoo. It is called "kvass," and was introduced by the Russians, though the Aleutian kvass is only a coarse imitation of the Russian article, as the Indian hootchenoo is of whiskey. In its manufacture they put a quantity of sugar and flour, or molasses and flour, with a few dried apples, in a cask, fill it up with water, and leave it to ferment. Then they make haste to drink it while it is yet thick and acrid, and capable of making them howling drunk. It also creates a fiery thirst for alcohol, which is supplied by traders whenever they get a chance. This renders the misery of the Aleuts complete.

There are about two thousand of them scattered along the chain of islands, living in small villages. Nearly all the men are hunters of the fur seal, the most expert making five hundred dollars or more per season. After paying old debts contracted with the Companies, they invest the remainder in trinkets, in clothing not so good as their own furs, and in beer, and go at once into hoggish dissipation, hair-pulling, wife-beating, etc. In a few years their health becomes impaired, they become less successful in hunting, their children are neglected and die, and they go to ruin generally. When they toss in their kayaks among surf-beaten rocks where their prey dwells, their business requires steady nerve. But all the proceeds are spent for what is worse than useless. The best hunters have been furnished with frame cottages by the Companies. These cottages have a neat appearance outside, but are very foul inside. Rare exceptions are those in which one finds scrubbed floors or flowers in pots on window-sills and mantels.

We called at the house of the priest of the Greek Church, and were received with fine civility, ushered into a room which for fineness of taste in furniture and fixtures might well challenge the very best in San Francisco or New York. The wallpaper, the ceiling, the floor, the pictures of Yosemite and the Czar on the walls, the flowers in the window, the books on the tables, the window-curtains white and gauzy, tied with pink ribbon, the rugs, and odds and ends, all proclaimed exquisite taste of a kind that could not possibly originate anywhere except in the man himself or his wife. This room would have made a keen impression upon me wherever found, and is, I am sure, not dependent upon the squalor of most other homes here, nor upon the wildness and remoteness of Una-laska, for the interest it excites. He spoke only Russian, so that I had but little conversation with him, as I had to speak through our interpreter. We smoked and smiled and gestured and looked at his beautiful home.

Bishop Nestor, who has charge of the Alaskan diocese, is said to be a charming and most venerable man. He now resides in San Francisco, but is having a house built in Unalaska. He is empowered to build and support, at the expense of the home church, a certain number of parish churches. Two out of seven of these are located among the Aleuts—at Unalaska and Belkofski. The other Aleutian villages which have churches, and nearly all have, build and support them at their own expense. The Russian Church claims about eleven thousand members in all Alaska. About one half of these are Aleuts, one thousand creoles, and the rest Indians of Nushagak, Yukon, and Kenai missions, over which the Church exercises but a feeble control. Shamanism with slight variations extends over all Siberia and Alaska and, indeed, all America.

2

Among the Islands
of Bering Sea

ST. PAUL, ALASKA, MAY 23, 1881   About four o'clock yesterday morning the Corwin left Unalaska, and arrived at St. Paul shortly after noon to-day, the distance being about one hundred and ninety miles. This is the metropolis of the Fur Seal Islands, situated on the island of St. Paul—a handsome village of sixty-four neat frame cottages, with a large church, school-house, and priest's residence, and a population of nearly three hundred Aleuts, and from twelve to twenty whites. It is interesting to find here an isolated group of Alaskan natives wholly under white influence and control, and who have in great part abandoned their own pursuits, clothing, and mode of life in general, and adopted that of the whites. They are all employed by the Alaska Commercial Company as butchers, to kill and flay the hundred thousand seals that they take annually here and at the neighboring island of St. George. Their bloody work lasts about two months, and they earn in this time from three hundred to six hundred dollars apiece, being paid forty cents per skin.

The Company supplies them with a school, medical attendance, and comfortable dwellings, and looks after their welfare in general, its own interest being involved. They even have a bank, and are encouraged to save their money, which many of them do, having accounts of from two hundred to three thousand dollars.

Among the Islands of Bering Sea

Fortunately, the Aleuts of St. Paul and St. George are pretty effectively guarded against whiskey, and to some extent against kvass also. Only limited quantities of sugar and other kvass material are sold to them. Nevertheless, one of their number told one of our officers to-day that he had a bank account of eight hundred dollars and would give it all for five bottles of whiskey; and an agent of the Company gave it as his opinion that there were not six perfectly sober Aleuts on the whole island to-day.

The number of fur seals that resort to these two islands, St. Paul and St. George, during the breeding season, is estimated at from three to four million, and there seems to be no falling off in numbers since the Alaska Commercial Company began operations here. Only young males are killed by the Company, but many of both sexes are taken far from here among the Aleutian Islands and around the shores of Vancouver Island and the outermost of the Alexander Archipelago.

No one knows certainly whence they come or whither they go. But inasmuch as they make their appearance every year about the shores of the Aleutian Islands shortly after their disappearance from St. Paul and St. George, and then later to the southward, toward the coast of British Columbia, it is supposed that they are the same animals, and that they thus make journeys every year of a thousand miles or more, and return to their birthplaces like shoals of salmon. They begin to appear on the breeding-grounds about the first of June. These are old males, who at once take up their stations on high ground a short distance from the shore, and keep possession of their places while they await the coming of the pregnant females who arrive about a month later, accompanied by the younger members of the community. At the height of the season the ground is closely covered with them, and they seldom go back into the water or take any food until the young are well grown and all are ready to leave the islands in the fall.

In addition to the one hundred thousand taken here, the Company obtains about forty thousand by purchase from the Russians at Bering and Copper Islands, and from Indians and traders at different points south as far as Oregon. These skins are said to be worth fifteen dollars apiece in the London market, to which they are all sent. The government revenue derived from the one hundred thousand killed each year is $317,000. Next in importance among the fur animals of Alaska is the sea-otter, of which about six thousand a year are taken, worth from eighty dollars to one hundred dollars apiece.

The Aleuts obtain from thirty to fifty dollars in goods or money, an alternative not due to the fact that the goods are sold for their money value, but to the fact that the traders sooner or later receive back whatever money they pay out instead of goods. Unlimited competition would, of course, run the price much higher, as, for example, it has done in southeastern Alaska. Here the only competition lies between the Western Fur and Trading Company and the Alaska Commercial Company. The latter gets most of them. Each company seeks the good-will of the best hunters by every means in its power, by taking them to and from the hunting grounds in schooners, by advancing provisions and all sorts of supplies, by building cottages for them, and supplying them with the services of a physician and medicine free. Only Indians are allowed by law to take furs, and whites married to Indian women. This law has induced some fifteen white men to marry Indians for the privilege of taking sea-otter. They have settled at Unga Island, one of the Shumagin group, where there is a village of some hundred and eighty-five Indians.

Among the Islands of Bering Sea

Seen from the sea, all the Pribilof Islands—St. Paul, St. George, and Otter Island—appear as mere rocks, naked and desolate fragments of lava, wasted into bluffs where they touch the sea, and shorn off on top by the ice-sheet. The gray surfaces are roughened here and there by what, at a distance, seem to be degraded volcanic cones. Nevertheless, they are exceedingly interesting, not only because of the marvelous abundance of life about them—seals, water birds, and fishes—but because they tell so grand a story concerning the ice-sheet that swept over them all from the north.

STEAMER CORWIN, TAPKAN, SIBERIA, MAY 31, 1881   On the twenty-fourth of this month, a bleak, snowy day, we enjoyed our first view of the northern ocean ice at a distance of only a few hours from the Pribilof Islands in latitude 58°. This is not far from its southern limit, though strong north winds no doubt carry wasting fragments somewhat farther. It always reaches lower on the American side. Norton Sound is seldom clear before the middle or end of June. Here the ice occurs in ragged, berglike masses from a foot to a hundred feet in breadth, and with the highest point not more than ten or twelve feet above the water. Its color is bluish-white, looking much like coarse, granular snow, with pale blue stratified bases under water.

We ran past one flat cake on which lay a small white seal which kept its place, though we were within fifteen or twenty feet of it. Guns were then brought into the pilot-house and loaded. In a few minutes another seal was discovered riding leisurely on its ice raft and shot. The engine was stopped, the boat lowered, and a sailor stepped on the ice and threw the heedless fellow into the boat. It seemed to pay scarce any attention to the steamer, and, when wounded by the first ball that was fired, it did not even then seek to escape, which surprised me since those among the fiords

[17]

north of Wrangell and Sitka are so shy that my Indians, as we glided toward them in a canoe, seldom were successful in getting a shot. The seal was nearly white—a smooth oval bullet without an angle anywhere, large, prominent, humanlike eyes, and long whiskers. It seemed cruel to kill it, and most wonderful to us, as we shivered in our overcoats, that it could live happily enough to grow fat and keep full of warm red blood with water at 32° F. for its pasture field, and wet sludge for its bed.

In half an hour we descried another, a large one, which we also shot as it lay at ease on a large cake against which the waves were beating. Like the other two, it waited until we were within easy range, and allowed itself to be shot without the slightest effort to escape. This one proved to be a fine specimen of the saddle-back species, *Histriophoca fasciata*, still somewhat rare in collections, and eagerly sought for. It derives its name from the saddlelike bands of brown across the back. This specimen weighed about two hundred pounds. The skins of both were saved, and the next morning we had some of the flesh of the small one for breakfast. The meat proved to be excellent, dark-red, and very tender, with a taste like that of good venison.

We were steering direct for St. Matthew Island, noted for the great numbers of polar bears that haunt its shores. But as we proceeded, the ice became more and more abundant, and at length it was seen ahead in a solid pack. Then we had to abandon our plan of landing on the island, and steered eastward around the curving edge of the pack across the mouth of Anadir Gulf.

On the twenty-seventh we sighted the Siberian coast to the north of the Gulf, snow-clad mountains appearing in clear outline at a distance of about seventy miles. Even thus far the traces of glacial action were easily recognized in the peculiar sculpture of the peaks, which here is as unmistakably marked as it is on the summits of the Sierra. Strange that this has not before attracted the attention of observers. The highest of the peaks seems to be perhaps four thousand feet above the sea. I hope I may yet have the chance to ascend them.

On the morning of the twenty-eighth we came to anchor near an Eskimo village at the northwest end of St. Lawrence Island. It was blowing and snowing at the time, and the poor storm-beaten row of huts seemed inexpressibly dreary through the drift. Nevertheless, out of them came a crowd of jolly, well-fed people, dragging their skin canoes, which they shoved over the rim of stranded ice that extended along the shore, and soon they were alongside the steamer, offering ivory, furs, sealskin boots, etc., for tobacco and ammunition.

There was much inquiry for beads, molasses, and most of all for rum and rifles, though they willingly parted with anything they had for tobacco and calico. After they had procured a certain quantity of these articles, however, nothing but rifles, cartridges, and rum would induce them to trade. But according to American law, these are not permitted to be sold. There seems to be no good reason why common rifles[1] should be prohibited, inasmuch as they would more surely and easily gain a living by their use, while they are peaceable and can hardly be induced to fight without very great provocation.

As to the alcohol, no restriction can possibly be too stringent. To the Eskimo it is misery and oftentimes quick death. Two years

---

[1] By a "common rifle" Muir probably meant a single-shot or muzzle-loading rifle. He changed his mind on this subject when he became aware of the excessive slaughter of caribou, or wild reindeer, committed by the natives with repeating rifles.

ago the inhabitants of several villages on this island died of starvation caused by abundance of rum, which rendered them careless about the laying up of ordinary supplies of food for the winter. Then an unusually severe season followed, bringing famine, and, after eating their dogs, they lay down and died in their huts. Last year Captain Hooper found them where they had died, hardly changed. Probably they are still lying in their rags. They numbered several hundreds.

When the people from this village came aboard to-day they said ours was the first ship of the season, and they were greatly delighted, running over the ship like children. We gave them lead, powder and caps, tobacco, et cetera, for ivory, arctic shoes, and reindeer parkas, in case we should need them for a winter in the ice, ordinary boots and woolen clothing being wholly inadequate. These are the first Eskimos that I have seen. They impress me as being taller and less distinct as a race than I had been led to suppose. They do not greatly differ from the Tlingits of southeastern Alaska; have Mongolian features well marked, seem to have less brain than the Tlingits, longer faces, and are more simple and childlike in behavior and disposition. They never quarrel much among themselves or with their neighbors, contrasting greatly in this respect with the Tlingits or Koluschans.

It was interesting to see how keenly and quickly they felt a joke, and winced when exposed to ridicule. Some of the women are nearly white. They show much taste in the manufacture of their clothing, and make everything durable. With their reindeer trousers, sack, shirt, and sealskin shoes they bid defiance to the most extreme cold. Their sack, made from the intestine of the sea-lion, while exceedingly light, is waterproof. Some of their parkas are made of the breast skins of ducks, but in no case do they wear blankets. When they can procure calico or drilling they wear over-shirts of this material, which gives them a very shabby and dirty look. Why they should want such flimsy and useless material I cannot guess. Dressed in their roomy furs, tied at the waist, they seem better-dressed than any other Indians I have seen. The trousers of the men are made of sealskin, with the fur outside. Those of the women are of deerskin and are extremely baggy. The legs, where gathered and tied below the knee, measure about two feet in diameter.

The chief of this village is a large man, five feet ten inches or six feet tall, with a very long flat face and abruptly tapering forehead, small, bright, cunning eyes, and childishly good-natured and wide-awake to everything curious. Always searching for something to laugh at, they are ready to stop short in the middle of most important bargainings to get hold of some bit of fun. Then their big faces would fall calm with ludicrous suddenness, either from being empty or from some business requiring attention. There was less apparent squalor and misery among them than among any other Indians I have seen.

It is a curious fact that they cut off their hair close to the scalp, all save a narrow rim around the base, much like the Chinese without the queue. The hair in color and coarseness is exactly like that of the Chinese; in a general way they resemble them also in their clothes. Their heads seem insensible to cold, for they bare them to the storms, and seem to enjoy it when the snow falls on their skulls. There is a hood, however, attached to most parkas, which is drawn up over the head in very severe weather.

Their mode of smoking is peculiar. The pipe is made of brass or copper, often curiously inlaid with lead, and the bowl is very small, not over a quarter of an inch in diameter inside, and with a flaring cuplike rim to prevent loss when it is being filled. Only a small pinch of finely pulverized tobacco is required to fill it. Then the Eskimo smoker lights it with a match, or flint and steel, and without removing the pipe from his mouth, sucks in the smoke and inhales it, inflating his lungs to the utmost and holding it a second or two, expels it, coughs, and puts his pipe and little bag of tobacco away, the whole smoke not lasting one minute. From the time he commences he holds his breath until it is finished. The more acrid and pungent the tobacco the better. If it does not compel them to cough and gasp it is not considered good. In buying any considerable quantity they try it before completing the bargain. This method of smoking is said to be practiced among all the Eskimos and also the Chukchis of Siberia.

In buying whiskey or rum from the traders it is said that they select one of their number to test its strength. The trader gives nearly pure alcohol, so that the lucky tester becomes drunk at once, which satisfies them. Then the keg that is purchased is found to be well watered and intoxication goes on slowly and feebly, much to their disgust and surprise.

3

Siberian Adventures

[STEAMER CORWIN, TAPKAN, SIBERIA, MAY 31, 1881] After inquiring about the movements of the ice and the whaling fleet, we weighed anchor and steered for Plover Bay on the coast of Siberia, taking several of the natives with us. They had a few poles for the frame of a boat and skins to cover it, and for food a piece of walrus flesh which they ate raw. This, with a gun and a few odds and ends, was all their property, yet they seemed more confident of their ability to earn a living than most whites on their farms.

The afternoon was clear and the mountains about Plover Bay showed themselves in bold relief, quite imposing and Yosemitic in sculpture and composition. There was so much ice at the mouth of the bay, which is a glacial fiord, that we could not enter. In the edge of the pack we spoke the whaler Rainbow, and delivered the Arctic mail. Then we proceeded a short distance northward, put into Marcus Bay, and anchored in front of a small Chukchi settlement. A boatful of natives came aboard and told a story "important if true," concerning the destruction of the lost whaler Vigilant and the death of her crew. Three Chukchi seal hunters, they said, while out on the ice last November, near Cape Serdzekamen, discovered the ship in the pack, her masts broken off by the ice, and the crew dead on the deck and in the cabin. They had brought off a bag of money and such articles as they could carry away, some of which had been shown to other natives, and the story had traveled from one settlement to another thus far down the coast.

The Cruise of the Corwin

All this was told with an air of perfect good faith, and they seemed themselves to believe what they were telling. We had heard substantially the same story at St. Lawrence Island. But knowing the ability of these people for manufacturing tales of this sort, we listened with many grains of allowance, though of course determined to investigate further.

Here we began to inquire for dogs, and were successful in hiring a team of six, and their owner to drive them. The owner is called "Chukchi Joe," and since he can speak a little English he is also to act in the capacity of interpreter, his language being the same as that spoken by the natives of the north Siberian coast. While we were trying to hire him, one of his companions kept reiterating that there was no use in sending out people to look for the crews of those ships, for they were all dead. Joe also said that it was no use going, and that he was afraid to venture so far for fear he would never get back. The snow, he objected, was too soft at this time of year, and many rivers hard to cross were in the way, and he did not like to leave his family. But after we had promised to pay him well, whether our lost friends were found or not, he consented to go, and when he went ashore to get ready we went with him.

The settlement consisted of only two habitations with twenty-five or thirty persons, located back three quarters of a mile from the coast. On reaching home Joe quickly vanished. His hut was about twenty-five feet in diameter, and was made of poles bent down at the top, where they all met to form a hemisphere. This frame was covered with skins of seal, sea-lion, and walrus, chiefly the latter. . . . Since much of the flesh on which the Chukchis subsist is eaten raw, only very small fires are made, and the huts are cold. The ground inside of this one was wet and muddy as a California corral in the rainy season, and seemed almost as large. But around the sides of this cold, squalid shell, little more than a wind-break and partial shelter from rain and snow, there were a number of very snug, clean, luxurious bedrooms, whose sides, ceiling, and floor were made of fur; they were lighted by means of a pan of whale-oil with a bit of moss for a wick. After being out all day hunting in the stormy weather, or on ice-packs or frozen tundras, the Chukchi withdraws into this furry sanctum, takes off all his clothing, and spreads his wearied limbs in luxurious ease, sleeping perfectly nude in the severest weather.

After introducing ourselves and shaking hands with a few of the most dignified of the old men, we looked about the strange domicile. Dogs, children, men, women, and utensils; spears, guns, whale-lances, etc., were stuck about the rafters and hanging on the supporting posts. We looked into one of the fur bedrooms, about six by seven, and found Joe enjoying a bath ere putting on his fine clothes to set out with us. Soon he emerged clad in a blue cloth army coat with brass buttons and shoulder straps and army cap! I scarcely knew him.

In the mean time Captain H[ooper] was off taking a drive over the snow with a dog-team and sled. When he returned Joe was having a farewell talk with his wife, who seemed very anxious about his safety and long absence. His little boy, too, about a year and a half old, had been told that his father was going away and he seemed to understand somewhat, as he kept holding him by the legs and trying to talk to him while looking up in his face. When we started away from the house he kissed his boy and bade him good-bye. The little fellow in his funny bags of fur toddled after him until caught and carried back by some of the women who were looking on. Joe's wife came aboard for a final farewell. After taking him aside and talking with him, the tears running down her cheeks, she left the vessel and went back with some others who had come to trade deerskins, while we sailed away. One touch of nature makes all the world kin, and here were many touches among the wild Chukchis.

We next proceeded to St. Lawrence Bay in search of furs and more dogs, and came to anchor at the mouth of the bay, opposite a small Chukchi settlement of two huts, at half-past one in the afternoon, May 29. This bay, like all I have seen along this coast, is of glacial formation, conducting back into glacial fountains in a range of peaks of moderate height. The wind was blowing hard from the south and snow was falling. The natives, however, came off at once to trade. Here we met the voluble Jaroochah, who sat gravely on the sloppy deck in the sludge, and told the story of the wrecked Vigilant in a loud, vehement, growling, roaring voice and with frantic gestures. He assured us over and over again that there was no use in going to seek any of the crew, for they were all dead and the ship with her broken masts had drifted away again to the north with the ice-pack. When told that we would certainly seek them whether dead or alive, he explained that the snow and ice were too soft for sleds at this time of year. Seeing that we were still unconvinced, he doubtless regarded us as foolish and incorrigible white trash.

We went ashore to fetch some dogs they offered to sell, but they changed their minds and refused to sell at any price, nor were they willing to barter deerskins that we needed for the trip and for winter clothing in case we should be caught in the ice and compelled to pass a winter in the Arctic. We presented them with a bucket of hardtack which no one of the party touched until the old orator gave orders to his son to divide it. This he did by counting it out on the deck, laying down one biscuit for each person and then adding one to each until all was exhausted, piling them on each other like a money-changer counting out coins. The mannerly reserve and unhasting dignity of all these natives when food is set before them is very striking as compared with the ravenous, snatching haste of the hungry poor among the whites. Even the children look wistfully at the heap of bread, without touching it until invited, and then eat very slowly as if not hungry at all. Nor do they ever need to be told to wait. Even when a year of famine occurs from any cause, they endure it with fortitude such as would be sought for in vain among the civilized, and after braving the most intense cold of these dreary ice-bound coasts in search of food, if unsuccessful, they wrap themselves in their furs and die quietly as if only going to sleep. This they did by hundreds two years ago on St. Lawrence Island.

Finding that we could not buy anything that we wanted here, savage eloquence being the only article offered, we sailed for the Diomedes. Here we found the natives eager to trade away everything they had. We bought a lot of furs and nineteen dogs, paying a sack of flour for each dog. This Arctic cattle market was in every way lively and picturesque, and ended satisfactorily to all the parties concerned. The scene of barter as each Eskimo, pitching alongside in his skin boat, hoisted the howling wolves aboard and thence to the upper deck in front of the pilot-house, was a rare one.

The villages are perched on the steep rocky slopes of mountains which drop at once sheer into deep water, one mountain per island.[1] No margin is left for a village along the shore, so, like the seabirds that breed here and fly about in countless multitudes dark-

---

[1]Muir noted in his journal that "Fairway Rock near the East Diomede is a similar smaller island, on which the granite rock is glaciated."

[27]

ening the water, the rocks, and the air, the natives had to perch their huts on the cliffs, dragging boats and everything up and down very steep trails. The huts are mostly built of stone with skin roofs. They look like mere stoneheaps, black dots on the snow at a distance, with whalebone posts set up and framed at the top to lay their canoes beyond the dogs that would otherwise eat them. The dreariest towns I ever beheld—the tops of the islands in gloomy storm-clouds; snow to the water's edge, and blocks of rugged ice for a fringe; then the black water dashing against the ice; the gray sleety sky, the screaming water birds, the howling wind, and the blue gathering sludge!

We now pushed on through the strait and into the Arctic Ocean without encountering any ice, and passed Cape Serdzekamen this afternoon [May 31]. The weather has been calm and tolerably clear for the last twenty-four hours, enabling us to see the coast now and then. It showed hills of moderate height, rising here and there to mountains.

About twelve miles northwest from Cape Serdzekamen we observed a marked bluff where the shore ice seemed narrower than elsewhere, and we approached, intending to examine it with reference to landing the party here. When we were within a mile of it we saw a group of natives signaling us to land by waving something over their heads. The Captain, Joe, and myself got on the ice from the boat, and began to scramble over it toward the bluff, but found the ice very rough and made slow progress. The pack is made up of a crushed mass of blocks and pinnacles tilted at every angle up to a height of from ten to thirty feet, and it seemed to become rougher and more impassable as we advanced.

Fortunately we discovered a group of natives a quarter of a

mile or so to the westward, coming toward the ship, when we returned to our boat that was lying at the edge of the ice, and went
around to meet them. After shaking hands with the most imposing
of the group of eight, we directed Joe to tell them the object we had
in coming, and to inquire whether two of their number would go
with our sledge party to assist in driving the teams. One of them, a
strapping fellow over six feet tall, said that he had a wife and four
boys and two girls to hunt seals for, and therefore could not go. As
Joe interpreted him in whaler English, he was "already hungry like
hell." Another said that the journey was too long for *him*, that our
friends were not along the coast, else he would certainly have heard
about them, and therefore the journey would be vain. We urged
that we were going to seek them whether they were to be found or
not, and that if they would go with us we would leave more food
for their families than they could get for them by hunting.

Two of the number at length consented to go, after being assured that we would pay them well, whether the journey proved
successful or otherwise. Then we intimated that we would like to
visit their village, which seemed to please them; for they started at
once to guide us over the hummocky ice to where they had left
their dog-teams and sleds. It was a rough scramble at best, and even
the natives slipped at times and hesitated cautiously in choosing a
way, while we, encumbered with overcoats and not so well shod,
kept sinking with awkward glints and slumps into hopper-shaped
hollows and chasms filled with snow. One of them kindly gave me
his balancing-stick.

Beyond the roughest portion of the hummock region we
found the dogs, nearly a hundred of them, with eleven sleds, making, as they lay at their ease, an imposing picture among the white

ice. Three of the teams were straightened out and one of them given in charge of Joe, who is an adept at driving, while the Captain and I were taken on behind the drivers of the other two; and away we sped over the frozen ceiling of the sea, two rows of tails ahead.

The distance to the village, called "Tapkan" by the natives, was about three miles, the first mile very rough and apparently hopelessly inaccessible to sleds. But the wolfish dogs and drivers seemed to regard it all as a regular turnpike, and jogged merrily on, up one side of a tilted block or slab and down the other with a sudden pitch and plunge, swishing round sideways on squinted cakes, and through pools of water and sludge in blue, craggy hollows, on and on, this way and that, with never a halt, the dogs keeping up a steady jog trot, and the leader simply looking over his shoulder occasionally for directions in the worst places. The driver admonished them with loud calls of "Hoora! Hoora! Shedack! Shedack! Knock! Knock!" but seldom struck them. He had to hold himself in constant readiness to jump off and hold the sled while guiding it around sharp angles and across the high cutting ridges. My sled was not upset at all, and the Captain's only twice.

Part of our way was across the mouth of a bay on smooth ice that had not been subjected to the mashing, upheaving strain of the ocean ice, and over this we glided rapidly. My Chukchi driver, now that he had no care about the upsetting of the sled, frequently turned with a smile and did his best to entertain me, though he did not understand a word of English. It was a rare, strange ride for us, yet accomplished with such everyday commonplace confidence, that it seemed at the time as if this might be the only mode of land travel in the world.

Some teams were just arriving from the village as we were

going to it. When we met, the dogs passed each other to right or left as they were told by their drivers, who kept flourishing a whip and jingling some iron rings that were tied loosely to one end of a short stick that had an iron goad in the other, and of which the dogs knew the use all too well. They are as steady as oxen, each keeping its trace-line tight, and showing no inclination to shirk—utterly unlike the illustrations I had seen, in which all are represented as running at a wild gallop with mouths wide open.

The village is built on a sand-bar pushed up by the ice on the west side of a narrow bay. I counted twenty huts in all. When we drove up, the women and children, and a few old men who had not been tempted to make the journey to the ship, came out to meet us. Captain Hooper went to the house belonging to his driver, I to the one belonging to mine; afterwards we joined and visited in company. We were kindly received and shown to good seats on reindeer skins. All of them smiled good-naturedly when we shook hands with them, and tried to repeat our salutations. When we discussed our proposed land journey the women eagerly joined and the children listened attentively.

We inquired about the Vega, knowing that she had wintered hereabouts. At first they said they knew nothing about her; that no ship had wintered here two years ago. Then, as if suddenly remembering, one of them said a three-masted ship, a steamer like the Corwin, had stopped one season in the ice at a point a few miles east of the village, and had gone away when it melted in the summer. A woman, who had been listening, then went to a box, and after turning it over, showed us a spoon, fork, and pocket compass of Russian manufacture, which she said the captain had given them.

The Cruise of the Corwin

The huts here are like those already described, only they are dry because of the porous character of the ground. Three or four families live in one, each having a private polog of deerskins, of which there are several thicknesses on the floor. We were shown into one—the snuggest storm nest imaginable, and perfectly clean. The common hut is far otherwise; dogs mingle with the food, hair is everywhere, and strangely persistent smells that defy even the Arctic frosts. The children seemed in fair ratio with the adults. When a child is to be nursed the mother merely pulls out one of her arms from the roomy sleeve of her parka and pushes it down until the breast is exposed. The breasts are pendulous and cylindrical, like those of the Tlingits.

The dishes used in domestic affairs are of wood, and in the smallest of these the puppies, after licking them, were often noticed to lie down. They seemed made specially for them, so well did they fit. Dogs were eagerly licking the large kettles, also, in which seal meat had been boiled. They seemed to be favored in these establishments like the pigs in Irish huts. Spears, lances, guns, and nets were fastened about the timbers of the roof and sides, but little food of any kind was visible. A pot was swinging over a small fire of driftwood when we entered one of the huts, and an old dame was stirring it occasionally, and roasting seal liver on the coals beneath it. On leaving we were each presented with a pair of fur mittens.

At the last moment, when we were ready to return to the ship, one of the men we had engaged to go with the land party changed his mind and concluded to stay at home. The other stuck to his engagement, though evidently feeling sore about leaving his family. His little boy cried bitterly when he learned that his father was going away, and refused all the offers made by the women to comfort him. After we had sped away over the ice, half a mile from the village, we could still hear his screams. Just as the ship was about to weigh anchor, the second man again offered to go with us, but Joe said to the Captain, "More better not take that fellow, he too much talk."

The group of lookers-on congregated on the edge of the ice was very picturesque seen from the vessel as we moved away. The Chukchis are taller and more resolute-looking people than the Eskimos of the opposite coast, but both are Mongols and nearly alike in dress and mode of life, as well as in religion.

The weather is promising this evening. No portion of the polar pack is in sight, and we mean to push on westward as far as we can with safety.

4

In Peril from the Pack

STEAMER CORWIN, NEAR THE EDGE OF THE SHORE ICE, OPPO-
SITE KOLIUCHIN ISLAND, 6 P.M., JUNE 2, 1881   After leaving
Tapkan, twelve miles northwest of Cape Serdzekamen, on the evening of the last day of May, we steamed along the coast to the
westward, tracing the edge of the shore-ice, which seemed to be
from three to six miles wide. The weather was tranquil, though
rather thick at times, and the water was like glass and as smooth as
a mill-pond. About half-past five yesterday afternoon we reached
the end of the open lead that we had been following, one hundred
and thirty miles west of Cape Serdzekamen, latitude 68° 28' N.,
longitude 175° 10' W., having thus early in the season gained a
point farther west than the Corwin was able to reach at any time
last year.

At this point the firm coast ice united with the great polar
pack, and, as there was danger of its drifting south at any time and
cutting us off, we made haste to the eastward, keeping as far offshore as possible, that we might be able to watch the movements
of the pack. About seven o'clock last evening, the weather becoming thick, the engine was stopped and the vessel was allowed to
proceed slowly under sail.

Shortly after one o'clock this morning I was awakened by unusual sounds on deck, and after listening for a few minutes, concluded that we must be entangled in the edge of the pack and were
unshipping the rudder for fear it might be carried away. Going on

[34]

deck, I was surprised to see the broken rudder being hoisted, for I had not been awakened by the blow. The oak shaft was broken completely off, and also all three of the pintles. It seems that about midnight, owing to the fog and snow, we got into a field of heavy masses of ice on the edge of the main pack, which, on account of a north wind that had commenced to blow, was now moving slowly southward, and while backing out of it, a moderate bump that chanced to take the rudder at the greatest disadvantage broke it off without any appreciable strain.

The situation was sufficiently grave and exciting—dark weather, the wind from the north and freshening every minute, and the vast polar pack pushing steadily shoreward. It was a cold, bleak, stormy morning, with a close, sweeping fall of snow, that encumbered the deck and ropes and nearly blinded one when compelled to look to windward. Our twenty-five dogs made an effective addition to the general uproar, howling as only Eskimo dogs can. They were in the way, of course, and were heartily kicked hither and thither. The necessary orders, however, were being promptly given and obeyed. As soon as the broken rudder was secured on deck, four long spars were nailed and lashed firmly together, fastened astern and weighted to keep them in place at the right depth in the water. This made a capital jury-rudder. It was worked by ropes attached on either side and to the steam windlass. The whole was brought into complete working order in a few hours, nearly everybody rendering service, notwithstanding the blinding storm and peril, as if jury-rudder making under just these circumstances were an everyday employment. Then, finding everything worked well, we made our escape from the closing ice and set out for Plover Bay to repair the damage.

About four in the afternoon, as the clouds lifted, we sighted

Koliuchin Island, which our two Chukchi natives hailed with joyful, beaming eyes. They evidently were uneasy because of the accident, and on account of being so long out of sight of land—a state of mind easily explained by the dangers attending their mode of life among the ice. In front of the island the ice seemed to be two or three miles wide and lavishly roughened with jammed, angular hummocks. Captain Hooper was now very anxious to get his sledge party landed. Everything was ready to be put on shore as soon as a safe landing-place should be discovered. The two Chukchis were in the pilot-house gazing wistfully at the gloomy snow-covered island as it loomed up in the gray, stormy sky with its jagged reach of ice in the foreground beaten by the waves.

The Captain directed Chukchi Joe, the interpreter, to ask his companion, the dog-driver, who was familiar with the condition of the ice on this part of the coast, whether this was a good point on which to land. His answer, as interpreted by Joe, was: "He says it's good; it's pretty good, he says." "Then get ready, Mr. Herring, for your journey," ordered the Captain. "Here, Quartermaster, get the provisions on deck." "Lower the boats there." "Joe, harness the dogs."

In a few minutes all was in readiness and in the boats. The party is composed of First Lieutenant Herring, in charge; Third Lieutenant Reynolds, a sailor[1] and the two Chukchis. They have twenty-five dogs, four sleds, a light skin boat to cross rivers and any open water they may find in their way, and two months' provisions. They were directed to search the coast as far to the westward as possible for the crew of the Jeannette or any tidings concerning the fate of the expedition; to interview the natives they met; to explore

---

[1]Coxswain Gessler.

the prominent portions of the coast for cairns and signals of any kind, and to return to Tapkan, where we would meet them, while in the mean time we propose to cruise wherever, under existing conditions, we can best carry out the objects of the expedition.

The party and all their equipments were carried from the vessel to the ice in three boats, roped together at intervals of twenty-five or thirty feet, the life-boat leading with the party, clothing, provisions, etc. Then came the dinghey, loaded nearly to the water's edge with the dogs, and one man to thrash them and keep some sort of order while they worried each other and raised an outrageous noise, on account of their uncomfortable, tumbled-together condition. And last, the skin boat, flying-light, with only the sleds aboard and one man to steer, the whole making a very extraordinary show.

Soon after the boats had left, while we were still watching the tossing fleet from the pilot-house and scanning the shore with reference to a landing-place, we noticed three dark objects on top of a hummock near the edge of the ice, and just back of them and to one side on a flat portion of the ice, a group of black dots. These proved to be three natives with their dog teams. They were out hunting seals, and had descried the ship with their sharp eyes and now came forward to gaze. This was a glad discovery to us, and no doubt still more so to the party leaving the ship, as they were now sure of the passable state of the ice, and would have guides with local knowledge to conduct them to the land. When the dogs got upon the ice, their native heath, they rolled and raced about in exuberant sport. The rough pack was home sweet home to them, though a more forbidding combination of sky, rough water, ice, and driving snow could hardly be imagined by the sunny civilized south.

The Cruise of the Corwin

After all were safely landed and our boats had returned, we went on our way, while the land party, busied about their sled-packing and dogs, gradually faded in the snowy gloom. All seems well this evening; no ice is in sight to the northward, and the jury-rudder is working extremely well.

[STEAMER CORWIN, EN ROUTE SOUTHWARD, TO PLOVER BAY.] JUNE 3   Snowing nearly all day. Cleared towards four in the afternoon. Spoke the Helen Mar; had taken five whales; another had already nine. Seven other whalers in sight, all of them save two smoking like steamers. They are trying out their abundant blubber; in danger of being blubber-logged. Saw an Indian[1] canoe leaving the Helen Mar as we approached; probably had been trading, the sea being smooth.

Had a good view of the two Diomedes; the western one is very distinctly glaciated, nearly all of the summit being comprehended in one beautiful ice-fountain, giving it a craterlike form. The residual glacial action, however, has been light, comparatively, here. No deep cañons putting back into the mountains, most of which are low. It is interesting, however, to see undoubted traces both of general and local glaciation thus far north, where the ground is in general rather low. Came up to the ice-pack about ten in the evening, so turned back and lay to.

JUNE 4   Calm, bland, foggy water, glassy and still as a mill-pond. Cleared so that one could see a mile ahead at ten o'clock, and we got under way. Sun nearly clear for the first day since coming into the Arctic. Mild, too, for it is 45° F. at noon; even seemed hot. The clouds lifted from the mountains, showing their bases and

---

[1]Mr. Muir often applies this term to the Bering Sea natives in general, whether Innuits or Chukchis.

slopes up to a thousand feet; summits capped. East Cape in fine view; high headland still streaked with snow nearly to the base; summit white at close range. All the coast for at least two hundred miles west of East Cape shows distinct glaciation, both general and local. Many glacier fountains well characterized. Indian village off here. Were boarded by three canoe loads of Indian seal hunters from East Cape village. They traded ivory and shoes, called "susy" by their interpreter. We were anxious to tell them about our sledge party and inquired of one who spoke a few words of English whether any of their number could speak good English. He seemed to think us very unreasonable, and said, "Me speak good." Got a female eider duck; very fat. In one of the canoes there was a very large seal, weighing perhaps four hundred pounds.

This has been by far the most beautiful and gentle of our Arctic days, the water perfectly glassy and with no swell, mirroring the sky, which shows a few blue cloudless spots, white as satin near the horizon, of beautiful luster, trying to the eyes. More whalers in sight. Gulls skimming the glassy level. Innumerable multitudes of eider ducks, the snowy shore, and all the highest mountains cloud-capped—a rare picture and perfectly tranquil and peaceful! God's love is manifest in the landscape as in a face. How unlike yesterday! In the evening a long approach to sunset, a red sky mingling with brown and white of the ice-blink. Growing colder towards midnight. There is no night at all now; only a partial gloaming; never, even in cloudy midnights, too dark to read. So for more than a week. Ice in sight, but hope to pass it by running a few miles to shore. Are now, at half-past eleven in the evening, beyond St. Lawrence Bay. Hope to get into Plover Bay to-morrow morning at six o'clock.

5

A *Chukchi* Orator

STEAMER CORWIN, ST. LAWRENCE BAY, SIBERIA, JUNE 6, 1881
Yesterday morning at half-past one o'clock, when we were within
twenty-five miles of Plover Bay, where we hoped to be able to repair
our rudder, we found that the ice-pack was crowding us closer and
closer inshore, and that in our partly disabled condition it would
not be safe to proceed farther. Accordingly we turned back and put
into St. Lawrence Bay, to await some favorable movement in the
ice.

We dropped anchor at half-past seven in the morning opposite
a small Chukchi settlement. In a few hours the wind began to blow
fresh from the north, steadily increasing in force, until at eight in
the evening it was blowing a gale, and we were glad that we were in
a good harbor instead of being out at sea, slashing and tumbling
about with a broken rudder among the wind-driven ice. It also
rained and snowed most of the afternoon, the blue and gray sleet
mingling in grand uproar with the white scud swept from the crests
of the waves, making about as stormy and gloomy an atmosphere
as I ever had the fortune to breathe. Now and then the clouds broke
and lifted their ragged edges high enough to allow the mountains
along the sides and around the head of the bay to be dimly seen,
not so dimly, however, as to hide the traces of the heavy glaciation
to which they have been subjected. This long bay, as shown by its
trends, its relation to the ice-fountains at its head and the sculpture

A *Chukchi* Orator

of its walls, is a glacial fiord that only a short time ago was the channel of a glacier that poured a deep and broad flood into Bering Sea, in company with a thousand others north and south along the Siberian coast. The more I see of this region the more I am inclined to believe that all of Bering Sea and Strait is a glacial excavation.

In a party of natives that came aboard soon after we had dropped anchor, we discovered the remarkable Chukchi orator, Jaroochah, whose acquaintance we made at the settlement on the other side of the bay, during our first visit, and who had so vividly depicted the condition of the lost whaler Vigilant. To-day, after taking up a favorable position in the pilot-house, he far surpassed his previous efforts, pouring forth Chukchi in overwhelming torrents, utterly oblivious of the presence of his rival, the howling gale.

During a sudden pause in the midst of his volcanic eloquence he inquired whether we had rum to trade for walrus ivory, whereupon we explained, in total abstinence phrase, that rum was very bad stuff for Chukchis, and by way of illustration related its sad effects upon the Eskimo natives of St. Lawrence Island. Nearly all the natives we have thus far met admitted very readily that whiskey was not good for them. But Jaroochah was not to be so easily silenced, for he at once began an anti-temperance argument in saloon-and-moderate-drinker style, explaining with vehement gestures that some whiskey was good, some bad; that he sometimes drank five cupfuls of the good article in quick succession, the effect of which was greatly to augment his happiness, while out of a small bottle of the bad one, a small glass made him sick. And as for whiskey or rum causing people to die, he knew, he said, that that was a lie, for he had drunk much himself, and he had a brother who had enjoyed a great deal of whiskey on board of whalers for many years, and that though now a gray old man he was still alive and happy.

This speech was warmly applauded by his listening companions, indicating a public opinion that offers but little hope of success for the efforts of temperance societies among the Chukchis. Captain Hooper, the surgeon, and myself undertook to sketch the orator, who, when he had gravely examined our efforts, laughed boisterously at one of them, which, in truth, was a slanderous caricature of even *his* countenance, villainous as it was.

In trading his ivory for supplies of some sort, other than alcohol, he tried to extract some trifling article above what had been agreed on, when the trader threatened to have nothing further to do with him on account of the trouble he was making. This set the old chief on his dignity, and he made haste to declare that he was a good and honorable man, and that in case the trade was stopped he would give back all he had received and go home, leaving his ivory on the deck heedless of what became of it. The woman of the party, perhaps eighteen years of age, merry and good-looking, went among the sailors and danced, sang, and joked with them.

The gale increased in violence up to noon to-day, when it began to abate slightly, and this evening it is still blowing hard. The Corwin commenced to drag her anchor shortly after midnight, when another that was kept in readiness was let go with plenty of chain, which held, so that we rode out the gale in safety. The whalers Francis Palmer and Hidalgo came into the bay last evening from Bering Strait and anchored near us. This morning the Hidalgo had vanished, having probably parted her cable.

Last evening a second party of natives came aboard, having

made their way around the head of the bay or over the ice. Both parties remained on board all night as they were unable to reach the shore in their light skin boats against the wind. Being curious to see how they were enduring the cold, I went on deck early. They seemed scarcely to feel it at all, for I found most of them lying on the deck amid the sludge and sleeping soundly in the clothes they wore during the day. Three of them were sleeping on the broken rudder, swept by the icy wind and sprinkled with snow and fragments of ice that were falling from the rigging, their heads and necks being nearly bare.

I inquired why their reindeer parkas were made without hoods, while those of the Eskimos of St. Lawrence Island had them; observing that they seemed far more comfortable in stormy weather, because they kept the head and neck warm and dry. They replied that they had to hunt hard and look quick all about them for a living, therefore it was necessary to keep their heads free; while the St. Lawrence Eskimos were lazy, and could indulge in effeminate habits. They gave the same reason for cutting off most of the hair close to the scalps, while the women wear the hair long.

One of their number was very dirty, and Captain Hooper, who is becoming interested in glacial studies, declared that he had discovered two terminal moraines in his ears. When asked why he did not wash himself, our interpreter replied, "Because he is an old fellow, and it is too much work to wash." This was given with an air of having explained the matter beyond further question. Considering the necessities of the lives they lead, most of these people seem remarkably clean and well-dressed and well-behaved.

The old orator poured forth his noisy eloquence late and early, like a perennial mountain spring, some of his deep chest tones sounding in the storm like the roar of a lion. He rolled his wolfish eyes and tossed his brown skinny limbs in a frantic storm of gestures, now suddenly foreshortening himself to less than half his height, then shooting aloft with jack-in-the-box rapidity, while his people looked on and listened, apparently half in fear, half in admiration. We directed the interpreter to tell him that we thought him a good man, and were, therefore, concerned lest some accident might befall him from so much hard speaking. The Chukchis, as well as the Eskimos we have seen, are keenly sensitive to ridicule, and this suggestion disconcerted him for a moment and made a sudden pause. However, he quickly recovered and got under way again, like a wave withdrawing on a shelving shore, only to advance and break again with gathered force.

The chief man of the second party from the other side of the bay is owner of a herd of reindeer, which he said were now feeding among the mountains at a distance of one sleep—a day's journey—from the head of a bay to the south of here. He readily indicated the position on a map that we spread before him, and offered to take us to see them on a sled drawn by reindeer, and to sell us as many skins and as much meat as we cared to buy. When we asked how many reindeer he had, all who heard the question laughed at the idea of counting so many. "They cover a big mountain," he said proudly, "and nobody can count them." He brought a lot of ivory to trade for tobacco, but said nothing about it until the afternoon. Then he signified his readiness for business after awakening from a sound sleep on the wet icy deck.

Shortly after we had breakfasted, the reindeer chief having intimated that he and his friends were hungry, the Captain ordered a large pot of tea, with hardtack, sugar, and molasses, to be served to them in the pilot-house. They ate with dignified deliberation, showing no unseemly haste, but eating rather like people accustomed to abundance. Jaroochah, who could hardly stem his eloquence even while eating, was particular about having his son invited in to share the meal; also, two boys about eight years old, giving as a reason, "they are little ones." We also called in a young woman, perhaps about eighteen years old, but none of the men present seemed to care whether she shared with them or not, and when we inquired the cause of this neglect, telling them that white men always served the ladies first, Jaroochah said that while girls were "little fellows" their parents looked after them, but when they grew big they went away from their parents with "some other fellow," and were of no more use to them and could look out for themselves.

Those who were not invited to this meal did not seem to mind it much, for they had brought with them plenty of what the whalers call "black skin"—the skin of the right whale—which is about an inch thick, and usually has from half an inch to an inch of blubber attached. This I saw them eating raw with hearty relish, snow and sludge the only sauce, cutting off angular blocks of it with butcher-knives, while one end of the tough black rubberlike mass was being held in the left hand, the other between their teeth. Long practice enables them to cut off mouthfuls in this way without cutting their lips, although they saw their long knives back and forth, close to their faces, as if playing the violin. They get the whale skin from the whalers, excepting the little they procure themselves. They hunt the whale now with lances and gear of every kind bought from the whalers, and sometimes succeed in killing a good many. They eat the carcass, and save the bone to trade to the whalers, who are eager to get it.

After the old orator left the steamer, the reindeer man accused him of being "a bad fellow, like a dog." He evidently was afraid that we were being fooled by his overwhelming eloquence into believing that he was a great man, while the precious truth to be impressed upon us was that he, the reindeer man, whose herd covers a big mountain, was the true chief. I asked his son, who speaks a little English, why he did not make a trip to San Francisco, to see the white man's big town. He replied, as many a civilized man does under similar circumstances, that he had a little boy, too little to be left, and too little to leave home, but that soon he would be a big fellow, so high, indicating the hoped-for stature with his hand, then he would go to San Francisco on some whale-ship, to see where all the big ships and good whiskey came from.

These [Chukchis] also had heard the story of the Vigilant. The reindeer man's son is going with us to Plover Bay to look after some of his father's debtors. He has been supplying them with tobacco and other goods on credit, and he thought it time they were paying up. His little boy, he told us, was sick—had a hot, sore head that throbbed, showing with his hand how it beat in aching pulses, and asked for medicine, which the surgeon gave him with necessary directions, greatly to his relief of mind, it seemed.

Around the shore opposite our anchorage the ground is rather low, where the ancient glacier that filled the bay swept over in smooth curves, breaking off near the shore, an abrupt wall from seventy to a hundred feet high. Against this wall the prevailing north winds have piled heavy drifts of snow that curve over the bluff at the top and slope out over the fixed ice along the shore from the base. The gale has been loosening and driving out past the vessel, without doing us any harm, large masses of the ice, capped with the edge of the drift. One large piece drifted close past the steamer

A *Chukchi* Orator

and immediately in front of a large skin canoe capable of carrying thirty men. The canoe, which was tied to the stern of the ship, we thought was doomed to be carried away. The owners looked wistfully over the stern, watching her fate, while the sailors seemed glad of the bit of excitement caused by the hope of an accident that would cost them nothing. Greatly to our surprise, however, when the berg, rough and craggy, ten or twelve feet high, struck her bow, she climbed up over the top of it, and, dipping on the other side, glided down with a graceful, launching swoop into the water, like a living thing, wholly uninjured. The sealskin buffer, fixed in front and inflated like a bladder, no doubt greatly facilitated her rise. She was tied by a line of walrus hide.

Now that the wind is abating, we hope to get away from here to-morrow morning, and expect to find most of the ice that stopped our progress yesterday broken up and driven southward far enough to enable us to reach Plover Bay without further difficulty.

6

Eskimos and Walrus

STEAMER CORWIN, PLOVER BAY, JUNE 15, 1881   We left our
anchorage in St. Lawrence Bay at four in the morning, June 7, and
steered once more for Plover Bay. The norther that had been blowing so long gave place to a light southerly breeze, and a gentle
dusting of snow was falling. In the afternoon the sea became
smooth and glassy as a mountain lake, and the clouds lifted, gradually unveiling the Siberian coast up to the tops of the mountains.
First the black bluffs, standing close to the water, came in sight;
then the white slopes, and then one summit after another until a
continuous range forty or fifty miles long could be seen from one
point of view, forming a very beautiful landscape. Smooth, dull,
dark water in the foreground; next, a broad belt of ice mostly white
like snow, with numerous masses of blue and black shade among
its jagged, uplifted blocks. Then a strip of comparatively low shore,
black and gray; and back of that the pure white mountains, with
only here and there dark spots, where the rock faces are too steep
for snow to lie upon. Sharp peaks were seen, fluted by avalanches;
glacier wombs, delicate in curve and outline as shells; rounded,
overswept brows and domes, and long, withdrawing valleys leading
back into the highest alpine groups, whence flowed noble glaciers
in imposing ranks into what is now Bering Sea.

   We had hoped the gale had broken and driven away the floe
that barred our way on the fifth [of June], but while yet thirty miles

Eskimos and Walrus

from the entrance of the bay we were again stopped by an immense field of heavy ice that stretched from the shore southeastward as far as the eye could reach. We pushed slowly into the edge of it a few miles, looking for some opening, but the man in the crow's nest reported it all solid ahead and no water in sight. We thereupon steamed out and steered across to St. Lawrence Island to bide our time.

While sailing amid the loose blocks of ice that form the edge of the pack, we saw a walrus, and soon afterward a second one with its young. The Captain shot and killed the mother from the pilot-house, and the dinghey was lowered to tow it alongside. The eyes of our Indian passengers sparkled with delight in expectation of good meat after enduring poor fare aboard the ship. After floating for eight or ten minutes she sank to the bottom and was lost—a sad fate and a luckless deed.

It was pitiful to see the young one swimming around its dying mother, heeding neither the ship nor the boat. They are said to be very affectionate and bold in the defense of one another against every enemy whatever. We have as yet seen but few, though in some places they are found in countless thousands. Many vessels are exclusively employed in killing them on the eastern Greenland coast, and along some portions of the coast of Asia. Here also, the whalers, when they have poor success in whaling, devote themselves to walrus hunting, both for the oil they yield and for the valuable ivory. The latter is worth from forty to seventy cents per pound in San Francisco, and a pair of large tusks weighs from eight to ten pounds.

Along all the coasts, both of Asia and of America, the natives hunt and kill this animal, which to them is hardly less important for food and other uses than the seals. A large walrus is said to weigh from one to two tons. Its tough hide is used for cordage, and to cover canoes. The flesh is excellent, while the ivory formerly was employed for spear heads and other uses, and is now an important article of trade for guns, ammunition, calico, bread, flour, molasses, etc. The natives now kill a good many whales, having obtained lances and harpoons from the whites. Bone, in good years, is more important than the ivory, and furs are traded, also, in considerable quantity. By all these means they obtain more of the white man's goods than is well used. They probably were better off before they were possessed of a single civilized blessing—so many are the evils accompanying them!

Our Chukchi passenger does not appear to entertain a very good opinion of the St. Lawrence natives. He advised the Captain to keep a close watch of those he allowed to come aboard. We asked him to-day the Chukchi name of ice, which he gave as "eigleegle." When we said that another of his people called it "tingting," he replied that that was the way poor common people spoke the word, but that rich people, the upper aristocratic class to which he belonged, called it "eigleegle." His father, being a rich man, had three wives; most of his tribe, he said, have only one.

At nine o'clock in the evening we were still more than an hour's run from St. Lawrence Island, though according to reckoning we should have reached the northeast end of the island at eight o'clock. We had been carried north about sixteen miles, since leaving St. Lawrence Bay, by the current setting through the Strait. The water, having been driven south by the north gale, was pouring north with greater velocity than ordinary. The sky was a mass of dark, grainless cloud, banded slightly near the northwest horizon; one band, a degree in breadth above the sun, was deep indigo, with a few short streaks of orange and red. We have not seen a star since leaving San Francisco, and have seen the sun perfectly cloudless only once! We came to anchor near the northwest end of the island about midnight.

The next day, the eighth of June, was calm and mild. A canoe with ten men and women came alongside this morning, just arrived from Plover Bay, on their way home. They made signs of weariness, having pulled hard against this heavy current. The distance is fifty miles. It is not easy to understand how they manage to find their way in thick weather, when it is difficult enough for seamen with charts and compass.

In trying to account for the observed similarity between the peoples of the opposite shores of Asia and America, and the faunas and floras, scientists have long been combating a difficulty that does not exist save in their own minds. They have suggested that canoes and ships from both shores either were wrecked and drifted from one to the other, or that natives crossed on the ice which every year fills Bering Strait. As to-day, so from time immemorial canoes have crossed for trade or mere pleasure, steering by the swell of the sea when out of sight of land. As to crossing on the ice, the natives tell me that they frequently go with their dog-sleds from the Siberian side to the Diomedes, those half-way houses along the route, but seldom or never from the Diomedes to the American side, on account of the movements of the ice. But, though both means of communication, assumed to account for distribution as it is found to exist to-day, were left out, land communication in any case undoubtedly existed, just previous to the glacial period, as far south as the Aleutian Islands, and northward beyond the mouth of the Strait.

While groping in the dense fogs that hang over this region,

sailors find their way at times by the flight of the innumerable sea-birds that come and go from the sea to the shore. The direction, at least, of the land is indicated, which is very important in the case of small islands. How the birds find *their* way is a mystery.

This canoe alongside was "two sleeps" in making the passage. Time, I suppose, is reckoned by sleeps during summer, as there is no night and only one day. They at once began to trade eagerly, seeming to fear that they would be left unvisited, now that the whalers have all gone to the Arctic. In the forenoon, after the natives had left, we took advantage of the calm weather to go in search of the wrecked Lolita, which went ashore last fall a few miles to the north of here. On the way we passed through a good deal of ice in flat cakes that had been formed in a deep still bay, sheltered from floating ice which jams and packs it. This ice did not seem to be more than two or three feet thick, possibly the depth to which it froze last winter less the amount melted and evaporated since spring commenced.

Walruses, in groups numbering from two to fifty, were lying on cakes of ice. They were too shy, however, to be approached within shooting range, though many attempts were made. Some of the animals were as bulky, apparently, as oxen. They would awaken at the sound of the vessel crunching through the loose ice, lift their heads and rear as high as possible, then drop or plunge into the water. The ponderous fellows took headers in large groups; twenty pairs of flippers sometimes were in the air at once. They can stay under water five or six minutes, then come up to blow. If they are near the ship they dive again instantly, going down like porpoises, always exposing a large curving mass of their body while dropping their heads, and, lastly, their flippers are stretched aloft for an instant. Sometimes they show fight, make combined attacks on boats, and defend one another bravely. The cakes on which they congregate are of course very dirty, and show to a great distance. Since they soon sink when killed in the water, they are hunted mostly on the ice, and, when it is rough and hummocky, are easily approached.

We were not successful in finding the Lolita, so we steamed back to our anchorage in the lee of a high bluff near the Eskimo village. Soon three or four canoes came alongside, loaded with furs, ivory, and whalebone. Molasses, which they carry away in bladders and seal skins, is with them a favorite article of trade. Mixed with flour and blocks of "black skin," it is esteemed, by Eskimo palates, a dish fit for the gods. A group of listeners laughed heartily when I described a mixture that I thought would be to their taste. They smacked their lips, and shouted "yes! yes!" One brought as a present to our Chukchi, the reindeer man's son, a chunk of "black skin" that, in color and odor, seemed to be more than a year old. He no doubt judged that our Chukchi, if not starving, was at least faring poorly on civilized trash.

A study of the different Eskimo faces, while important trades were pending, was very interesting. They are better behaved than white men, not half so greedy, shameless, or dishonest. I made a few sketches of marked faces. One, who received a fathom of calico more than was agreed upon, seemed extravagantly delighted and grateful. He was lost in admiration of the Captain, whose hand he shook heartily.

We continued at anchor here the following day, June 9. It was snowing and the decks were sloppy. Several canoe loads of Eskimos came aboard, and there was a brisk trade in furs, mostly reindeer hides and parkas for winter use; also fox [skins] and some whale-bone and walrus ivory. Flour and molasses were the articles most in demand. Some of the women, heedless of the weather, brought their boys, girls, and babies. One little thing, that the proud mother held up for our admiration, smiled delightfully, exposing her two precious new teeth. No happier baby could be found in warm parlors, where loving attendants anticipate every want and the looms of the world afford their best in the way of soft fabrics. She looked gayly out at the strange colors about her from her bit of a fur bag, and when she fell asleep, her mother laid her upon three oars that were set side by side across the canoe. The snowflakes fell on her face, yet she slept soundly for hours while I watched her, and she never cried. All the youngsters had to be furnished with a little bread which both fathers and mothers begged for them, say-ing, "He *little* fellow, *little* fellow."

Four walrus heads were brought aboard and the ivory sold, while the natives, men and women, sat down to dine on them with butcher-knives. They cut off the flesh and ate it raw, apparently with good relish. As usual, each mouthful was cut off while held between the teeth. To our surprise they never cut themselves. They seemed to enjoy selecting tidbits from different parts of the head, turning it over frequently and examining pieces here and there, like a family leisurely finishing the wrecked hull of a last day's din-ner turkey.

These people interest me greatly, and it is worth coming far to know them, however slightly. The smile, or, rather, broad grin of that Eskimo baby went directly to my heart, and I shall remember it as long as I live. When its features had subsided into perfect repose, the laugh gone from its dark eyes, and the lips closed over

Eskimos and Walrus

its two teeth, I could make its sweet smile bloom out again as often as I nodded and chirruped to it. Heaven bless it! Some of the boys, too, lads from eight to twelve years of age, were well-behaved, bashful, and usually laughed and turned away their faces when looked at. But there was a response in their eyes which made you feel that they are your very brothers.

7

At Plover Bay
and St. Michael

STEAMER CORWIN, PLOVER BAY, JUNE 15, 1881   A little before
four o'clock the next morning, June 10, I was awakened by the
officer of the deck coming into the cabin and reporting that the
weather was densely foggy, and that ice in large masses was crowding down upon us, which meant "The Philistines be upon thee,
Samson!" Shortly afterward, the first mass struck the ship and
made her tremble in every joint; then another and another, in
quick succession, while the anchor was being hurriedly raised.
The situation in which we suddenly found ourselves was quite serious. The ice, had it been like that about the ship of the Ancient
Mariner, "here and there and all around," would have raised but
little apprehension. But it was only on one side of us, while a rocky
beach was close by on the other, and against this beach in our
disabled condition the ice was steadily driving us. Whether backing or going ahead in so crowded a bit of water, the result for some
time was only so many shoves toward shore.

At length a block of small size, twenty or thirty feet in diameter, drifted in between the Corwin and the shore, and by steaming
against it and striking it on the landward bow she glinted around,
head to the pack, and an opening allowed her to enter a little distance. This was gradually increased by stopping and starting until

we were safe in the middle of it. Watching the compass and constantly taking soundings, we traced the edge of the pack, and in an hour or two made our escape into open water.

After the fog lifted we went again in search of the Lolita, and discovered her five or six miles below the Eskimo village. Dropping anchor at the edge of a sheet of firm shore-ice, we went across it to the wreck to see whether we could not get some pintles from it for our rudder. We found her rudder had been carried away, but procured some useful iron, blocks, tackle, spars, etc.; also, two barrels of oil which the natives had not yet appropriated. The transportation of these stores to the ship over ice, covered with sludge and full of dangerous holes, made a busy day for the sailors.

Back a hundred yards from the beach I found a few hints of the coming spring, though most of the ground is still covered with snow. The dwarf willow is beginning to put out its catkins, and a few buds of saxifrages, erigerons, and heathworts are beginning to swell. The bulk of the vegetation is composed of mosses and lichens. Half a mile from the wreck there is a deserted Eskimo village. All its inhabitants are said to have died of famine two winters ago. The traces of both local and general glaciation are particularly clear and telling on this island.

In the afternoon, the weather being calm and mild, we succeeded in mending and shipping the rudder, and the next morning we set out yet again for Plover Bay, where we now are, having arrived about midnight on the eleventh. The men have been busy sawing and blasting a sort of slip in the ice for the ship that she may be secure from drift ice and well situated for loading the coal that is piled on the shore opposite here. The coal belongs to the Russians. In loading, the coal was first stowed well forward in order to lift the stern high enough out of water to enable us to make the additional repairs required on the rudder, since we cannot find access to a beach smooth enough to lay her on.

The Indians here are very poor. They have offered nothing to trade. With a group of men and women that came to the ship a few mornings ago there was a half-breed girl about two years old. She had light-brown hair, regular European features, and was very fair and handsome. Her mother, a Chukchi, died in childbirth, and the natives killed her father. She is plump, red-cheeked, and in every way a picture of health. That in a Chukchi hut, nursed by a Chukchi mother-in-law, and on Chukchi food, a half-European girl can be so beautiful, well-behaved, happy, and healthy is very notable.

On the twelfth of June we had snow, rain, and sleet nearly all day. The view up the inlet was very striking—lofty mountains on both sides rising from the level of the water, and proclaiming in telling characters the story of the inlet's creation by glaciers that have but lately vanished. Most of the slopes and precipices seemed particularly dreary, not only on account of the absence of trees, but of vegetation of any kind in any appreciable amount. No bits of shelf gardens were to be seen, though not wholly wanting when we came to climb, for I discovered some lovely garden spots with a tellima and anemone in full bloom. [The vegetation was] very dwarfed, and sparse, and scattered. No green meadow-hollows. The rock was fast disintegrating, and all the mountains appeared in general views like piles of loose stones dumped from the clouds. Plover Bay[1] takes its name from H.M.S. Plover, which passed the

---

[1]Called Providence Bay on recent maps.

winter of 1848–49 here while on a cruise in search of Franklin. It is a glacial fiord, which in the height of its walls is more Yosemite-like than any I have yet seen in Siberia.

In the afternoon Dr. Rosse and I set out across the ice to the cliffs. We found a great many seal holes and cracks of a dangerous kind, and a good deal of water on top of the ice that made the walking very sloppy. There were dog-sled tracks trending up and down the inlet. The ice is broken along the shore by the rise and fall of the tides, but we made out to cross on some large cakes wedged together. Just before we reached the edge of rocks, in scanning the ruinous, crumbling face of the cliffs that here are between two and three thousand feet high, I noticed an outstanding buttress harder and more compact in cleavage than the rest, and very obviously grooved, polished, and scratched by the main vanished glacier that once filled all the fiord. Up to this point we climbed, and found several other spots of the old glacial surface not yet weathered off. This is the first I have seen of this kind of glacial traces.

On the thirteenth the whaler Thomas Pope[1] arrived here and anchored to the ice near us. Getting everything in trim for the return voyage, having already taken all the [whale]-oil she can carry. All the fleet are doing well this year, or, as the natives express it, they are getting a "big grease."

[According to brief entries in Muir's journal the fourteenth, fifteenth, and sixteenth of June were spent aboard the Corwin, writing personal letters and several communications to the "San Francisco Bulletin." From Captain Hooper's report of the cruise of

[1]Captain M. V. B. Millard.

the Corwin, the following interesting record of events during the interval is extracted:—

> On the fourteenth we worked all day, drawing coal on the sleds, assisted by the natives and two sleds with three dogs each, but the rapidly melting ice made it very tedious. On the fifteenth we continued work, although the softness of the ice compelled us to reduce the loads to one-half their former size. About four in the afternoon a slight roll of the vessel was perceptible, indicating a swell coming in from the outside. At the same time a slight undulating motion of the ice was observed. This was followed by cracks in the ice running in every direction, and we had barely time to take in our ice anchors, call our men on board, and take the Thomas Pope in tow before the ice was all broken and in motion and rapidly drifting toward the mouth of the bay. At first it looked as if we might have to go to sea to avoid it. The wind by this time was blowing fresh from the northeast with a thick snow-storm, and, judging from the roll coming into the bay, a heavy sea must be running. Added to this was the fact of the sea being filled with large fields of heavy drift ice, making the prospect anything but a pleasing one. After lying off outside the ice for an hour or two and just when it seemed as if our only hope was in putting to sea, Captain Millard reported from the masthead that the whole body of ice had started offshore, and that if we could get in through it we could find good anchorage in clear water. Although

the ice was pitching and rolling badly, it was well broken up, and we determined to make the attempt, and succeeded better than I had anticipated, and about midnight we came out into clear water, and anchored near the shore in twelve fathoms, the Thomas Pope coming to just outside of us in twenty fathoms.

Muir's journal continues with the following record under date of June 17:]

Half-clear in the morning, foggy in the afternoon. Left Plover Bay at six in the morning with Thomas Pope[1] in tow. Left her at the mouth of the bay. It was barred with rather heavy ice, which was heaving in curious commotion from a heavy swell. We gave and received three cheers in parting. Have had a very pleasant time with Captains Millard and Kelly. Very telling views of the sculpture of the mountains along the Bay, at its head, and at the mouth, where the land-ice flowed into the one grand glacier that filled Bering Strait and Sea. The fronting cliffs of the sea glacier seem to be hardly more weathered than those of Plover Bay and adjacent fiords.

ST. MICHAEL, ALASKA, JUNE 20, 1881   Sunshine now in the Far North, sunshine all the long nightless days! ripe and mellow and hazy, like that which feeds the fruits and vines! We came into it two days ago when we were approaching this old-fashioned Russian trading post near the mouth of the Yukon River. How sweet and kindly and reviving it is after so long a burial beneath dark, sleety storm clouds! For a whole month before the beginning

---

[1] The *San Francisco Bulletin*, in its issue of July 13, 1881, noted the arrival in port of the whaling bark Thomas Pope with a series of letters from John Muir.

of this bright time, it snowed every day more or less, perhaps only for an hour or two, or all the twenty-four hours; not one day on which snow did not fall either in wet, sleety blasts, making sludge on the deck and rigging and afterward freezing fast, or in dry crystals, blowing away as fast as it fell. I have never before seen so cloudy a month, weather so strangely bewildering and depressing. It was all one stormy day, broken here and there by dim gleams of sunlight, but never so dark at midnight that we could not read ordinary print.

The general effect of this confusing interblending of the hours of day and night, of the quick succession of howling gales that we encountered, and of dull black clouds dragging their ragged, drooping edges over the waves, was very depressing, and when, at length, we found ourselves free beneath a broad, high sky full of exhilarating light, we seemed to have emerged from some gloomy, icy cave. How garish and blinding the light seemed to us then, and how bright the lily-spangles that flashed on the glassy water! With what rapture we gazed into the crimson and gold of the midnight sunsets!

While we were yet fifty miles from land a small gray finch came aboard and flew about the rigging while we watched its movements and listened to its suggestive notes as if we had never seen a finch since the days of our merry truant rambles along the hedgerows. A few hours later a burly, dozing bumblebee came droning around the pilot-house, seeming to bring with him all the warm, summery gardens we had ever seen.

The fourth of June was the most beautiful of the days we spent in the Arctic Ocean. The water was smooth, reflecting a tranquil, pearl-gray sky with spots of pure azure near the zenith and a belt of white around the horizon that shone with a bright, satiny luster, trying to the eyes like clear sunshine. Some seven whale-ships were in sight, becalmed with their canvas spread. Chukchi hunters in pursuit of seals were gliding about in light skin-covered canoes, and gulls, auks, eider ducks, and other water birds in countless multitudes skimmed the glassy level, while in the background of this Arctic picture the Siberian coast, white as snow could make it, was seen sweeping back in fine, fluent, undulating lines to a chain of mountains, the tops of which were veiled in the shining sky. A few snow crystals were shaken down from a black cloud towards midnight, but most of the day was one of deep peace, in which God's love was manifest as in a countenance.

The average temperature for most of the month commencing May twentieth has been but little above the freezing point, the maximum about 45° F. To-day the temperature in the shade at noon is 65°, the highest since leaving San Francisco. The temperature of the water in Bering Sea and Strait, and as far as we have gone in the Arctic, has been about from 29° to 35°. But as soon as we approached within fifty miles of the mouths of the Yukon, the temperature changed suddenly to 42°.

The mirage effects we have witnessed on the cruise thus far are as striking as any I ever saw on the hot American desert. Islands and headlands seemed to float in the air, distorted into the most unreal, fantastic forms imaginable, while the individual mountains of a chain along the coast appeared to dance at times up and down with a rhythmic motion, in the tremulous refracting atmosphere. On the northeast side of Norton Sound I saw two peaks, each with a flat, black table on top, looming suddenly up and sinking again alternately, like boys playing see-saw on a plank.

The trading post of St. Michael was established by the Russians in 1833. It is built of drift timber derived from the Yukon, and situated on a low bluff of lava on the island of St. Michael, about sixty-five miles northeast of the northmost of the Yukon mouths. The fort is composed of a square of log buildings and palisades, with outlying bastions pierced for small cannon and musketry, while outside the fort there are a few small buildings and a Greek church, reinforced during the early part of the summer with groups of tents belonging to the Indians and the traders. The fort is now occupied by the employees of the Alaska Commercial Company. This is the headquarters of the fur traders of northern and central Alaska.

The Western Fur and Trading Company has a main station on the side of the bay about three miles from here, and the two companies, being in close competition, have brought on a condition of the fur business that is bitterly bewailed by the subtraders located along the Yukon and its numerous tributaries. Not only have the splendid profits of the good old times diminished nearly to zero, say they, but the big prices paid for skins have spoiled the Indians, making them insolent, lazy, and dangerous, without conferring any substantial benefit upon them. Since they can now procure all the traders' supplies they need for fewer skins than formerly, they hunt less, and spend their idle hours in gambling and quarreling.

The furs and skins of every kind derived annually from the Yukon and Kuskoquim regions, and shipped from here, are said to be worth from eighty thousand to one hundred thousand dollars. The trade goods are brought to this point from San Francisco by the rival companies in June, and delivered to their agents, by

At Plover Bay and St. Michael

whom they are distributed to their traders and taken up the rivers to the different stations in the interior in boats towed most of the way by small stern-wheel steamers. Then, during the winter, the furs are collected and brought to this point and carried to San Francisco by the vessels that bring the goods for the next season's trade.

On the nineteenth instant the steamer belonging to the Western Fur and Trading Company arrived from a station fifteen hundred miles up the river, towing three large boats laden with Indians and traders, together with the last year's collection of furs. After they had begun to set up their tents and unload the furs, we went over to the storerooms of the Company to look at the busy throng. They formed a strange, wild picture on the rocky beach; the squaws pitching the tents and cutting armfuls of dry grass to lay on the ground as a lining for fur carpets; the children with wild, staring eyes gazing at us, or, heedless of all the stir, playing with the dogs; groups of dandy warriors, arrayed in all the colors of the rainbow, grim, and cruel, and coldly dignified; and a busy train coming and going between the warehouse and the boats, storing the big bundles of shaggy bearskins, black and brown, marten, mink, fox, beaver, otter, lynx, moose, wolf, and wolverine, many of them with claws spread and hair on end, as if still fighting for life. They were vividly suggestive of the far wilderness whence they came—its mountains and valleys, its broad grassy plains and far-reaching rivers, its forests and its bogs.

The Indians seemed to me the wildest animals of all. The traders were not at all wild, save in dress, but rather gentle and subdued in manners and aspect, like half-paid village ministers. They held us in a long interesting conversation, and gave us many valuable facts concerning the heart of the Yukon country. Some

Indians on the beach were basking in the yellow, mellow sun. Herring and salmon were hanging upon frames or lying on the rocks—a lazy abundance of food that discouraged thought of the future.

The shores here are crowded with immense shoals of herring, and the Indians are lazily catching just enough to eat. Those we had for dinner are not nearly so good as those I ate last year at Cross Sound. The Yukon salmon, however, are now in excellent condition, and are the largest by far that I have seen. Yet the Yukon Indians suffer severely at times from famine, though they might dry enough in less than a week to last a year.

We are making a short stay here to take on provisions, and intend to go northward again to-morrow to meet the search party that we landed near Koliuchin Island. Another delightful sunday—nearly cloudless and with lily-spangles on the bay. The temperature was 65° F. in the shade at noon. The birds are nesting and the plants are rapidly coming into bloom.

8

Return of the Search Party

After leaving St. Michael, on the evening of the twenty-first, we crossed Bering Sea to Plover Bay to fill our coal-bunkers from a pile belonging to His Majesty, the Czar of Russia.

On the twenty-third we were sailing along the north side of St. Lawrence Island against a heavy wind. There was a rough sea and a clear sky, save on the island. I had a tolerably clear view of the most prominent portion of the island near the middle. It is here composed of lava, reddish in color and dotted with craters and cones, most of which seem recent, though a slight amount of glaciation of a local kind is visible. About three in the afternoon we came to anchor off the northwest end of the island opposite the village. A few natives came aboard at eight o'clock.

The next day we got under way at four in the morning, going east along the south side of St. Lawrence Island. The norther again was blowing as hard as ever. We discovered an Eskimo village, but the natives were mostly dead. Coming to anchor there at six in the evening, we went ashore and met a few Eskimos who, though less demonstrative, seemed quite as glad to see us as those on the northwest end of the island. The village, as we examined it through our glasses, seemed so still and desolate, we began to fear that, like some of the villages on the north side of the island, not a soul was left alive in it, until here and there a native was discovered on the brow of the hill where the summer houses are.

After we had landed from the life-boat, two men and a boy came running down to meet us and took us up to the two inhabited houses. They all gathered about us from scattered points of observation, and when we asked where all the people were to whom the other houses belonged, they smiled and said, "All mucky." "All gone." "Dead?" "Yes, dead!" We then inquired where the dead people were. They pointed back of the houses and led us to eight corpses lying on the rocky ground. They smiled at the ghastly spectacle of the grinning skulls and bleached bones appearing through the brown, shrunken skin.

Being detained on the twenty-fifth by the norther which was still blowing, we went ashore after breakfast, and had a long walk through graves, back to noble views of the island, telling the grandeur of its glaciation by the northern ice-sheets. Weighed anchor and steered for Plover Bay shortly after nine in the evening, and arrived there early on the morning of the twenty-sixth. While the ship was being coaled, I climbed the east wall of the fiord three or four miles above the mouth, where it is about twenty-two hundred feet above the level of the sea, and, as the day was clear, I obtained capital views of the mountains on both sides and around the head of the fiord among the numerous ice-fountains which, during the glacial winter, poured their tribute through this magnificent channel into Bering Sea.

When the glacier that formed what is now called Plover Bay was in its prime, it was about thirty miles long and from five to six miles in width at the widest portion of the trunk, and about two thousand feet deep. It then had at least five main tributaries, which, as the trunk melted towards the close of the ice period, became independent glaciers, and these again were melted into perhaps seventy-five or more small residual glaciers from less than a mile to several miles in length, all of which, as far as I could see, have at length vanished, though some wasting remnants may still linger in the highest and best-protected fountains above the head of the fiord. I had a fine glissade down the valley of a tributary glacier whose terminal moraines show the same gradual death as those of the Sierra. The mountains hereabouts, in the forms of the peaks, ridges, lake-basins, bits of meadow, and in sculpture and aspects in general, are like those of the high Sierra of California where the rock is least resisting.

Snow still lingers in drift patches and streaks and avalanche heaps down to the sea-level, while there is but little depth of solid snow on the highest peaks and ridges, so that, there being no warm, sunny base of gentle slopes and foothills, no varying belts of climate, this region as a whole seems to consist of only the storm-beaten tops of mountains shorn off from their warm, well-planted bases. Still there are spots here and there, where the snow is melted, that are already cheered with about ten species of plants in full bloom: anemones, buttercups, primulas, several species of draba, purple heathworts, phlox, and potentilla, making charming alpine gardens, but too small and thinly planted to show at a distance of more than a few yards, while trees are wholly wanting.

On our way north to-day we stopped a few minutes opposite a small native settlement, six or eight miles to the northeast of the mouth of Metchigme Bay, in search of Omniscot, the rich reindeer owner, whom we had met further up the coast two weeks ago, and who had then promised to have a lot of deerskins ready for us if we would call at his village.

Some of the natives, coming off to the steamer to trade, informed us that Omniscot lived some distance up the bay that we had just passed, and one of them, who speaks a little English, inquired why we had not brought back Omniscot's son. He told us that he was his cousin and that his mother was crying about him last night, fearing that he would never come back.

We informed him that his cousin was crazy and had tried to kill himself, but that he was now at Plover Bay with one of his friends and would probably be home soon. This young Omniscot, whom we had taken aboard at St. Lawrence Bay, thinking that he might be useful as an interpreter, is a son of the reindeer man and belongs to the Chukchi tribe. We soon came to see that we had a troublesome passenger, for the expression of his eyes, and the nervous dread he manifested of all the natives wherever we chanced to stop, indicated some form of insanity. He would come to the door of the cabin to warn the Captain against the people of every village that we were approaching as likely to kill us, and then he would hide himself below deck or climb for greater safety into the rigging.

On the twenty-fifth, when we were lying at anchor off St. Lawrence Island, he offered his rifle, which he greatly prized, to one of the officers, saying that inasmuch as he would soon die he would not need it. He also sent word to the Captain that he would soon be "mucky," but came to the cabin door shortly afterward, with nothing unusual apparent in his face or behavior, and began a discussion concerning the region back of St. Michael as a location for a flock of reindeer. He thought they would do well there, he said, and that his father would give him some young ones to make a beginning, which he could take over in some schooner, and that they would get plenty of good moss to eat on the tundra, and multiply fast until they become a big herd like his father's, so big that nobody could count them.

In three or four hours after this he threw himself overboard, but was picked up and brought on deck. Some of the sailors stripped off his wet furs, and then the discovery was made that before throwing himself into the sea the poor fellow had stabbed himself in the left lung. The surgeon dressed his wound and gave as his opinion that it would prove fatal. He was doing well, however, when we left him, and is likely to recover. The Plover Bay natives, in commenting on the affair, remarked that the St. Lawrence people were a bad, quarrelsome set, and always kept themselves in some sort of trouble.

Having procured a guide from among the natives that came aboard here, we attempted to reach Omniscot's village, but found the bay full of ice, and were compelled to go on without our winter supply of deerskins, hoping, however, to be able to get them on the east coast.

There is quite a large Chukchi settlement near the mouth of the bay, on the north side. Seven large canoe-loads of the population came aboard, making quite a stir on our little ship. They are the worst-looking lot of Siberian natives that I have yet seen, though there are some fine, tall, manly fellows amongst them. Mr. Nelson, a naturalist, and zealous collector for the Smithsonian Institution, who joined us at St. Michael, photographed a group of the most villainous of the men, and two of the women whose arms were elaborately tattooed up to their shoulders. Their faces were a curious study while they were trying to keep still under circumstances so extraordinary.

The glaciation of the coast here is recorded in very telling characters, the movement of the ice having been in a nearly south-southwest direction. There is also a considerable deposit of irregularly stratified sand and gravel along this part of the coast. For fifteen or twenty miles it rises in crumbling bluffs fifty feet high, and makes a flat, gently sloping margin, from one hundred yards to several miles in width, in front of the mountains. The bay, moreover, is nearly closed by a bar, probably of the same material. The weather is delightful, clear sunshine, only a few fleecy wisps of cloud in the west, and the water still as a mill-pond.

JUNE 28   Anchored an hour or two this forenoon at the west Diomede, and landed a party to make observations on the currents and temperature of the water that sets through Bering Strait. Then proceeded on our way direct to Tapkan to seek our search party. The fine weather that we have enjoyed since the day before our arrival at St. Michael ended in the old, dark, gloomy clouds and drizzling fog on reaching the Diomedes, though the coast above East Cape has until now been in sight most of the time up to a height of about a thousand feet.

The glaciation, after the melting of the ice-sheet, has been light, sculpturing the mountains into shallow, short valleys and round ridges, mostly broad-backed. The valleys, for the most part, are not cut down to the sea. The shore seems to have been cut off by the glacier sheet that occupied the sea, after it was too shallow to flow over the angle of land formed by East Cape. This overflow is well marked, fifteen to twenty-five miles northwest of the Cape, in the trends of the ridges and valleys as far back as I could see, that is, about twenty-five miles from the shore. The north wind is, and has been, blowing for twenty-four hours, and we fear that we will soon meet with the drifting ice from the main polar pack.

Return of the Search Party

STEAMER CORWIN, OFF THE CHUKCHI VILLAGE OF TAPKAN, NEAR CAPE SERDZEKAMEN, SIBERIA, JUNE 29, 1881 We arrived here about eight this morning to meet the search party that we landed about a month ago, near Koliuchin Island. They had been waiting for us nearly two weeks. We were unable to land on account of the stormy weather, but after waiting about two hours we saw them making their way out to the edge of the drift ice, which extended about three miles from shore, and after a good deal of difficulty they reached the steamer in safety. The air was gray with falling snow, and the north wind was blowing hard, dashing heavy swells, with wild, tumultuous uproar, against jagged, tumbling ice blocks that formed the edge of the pack. The life-boat was lowered and pulled to the edge of the pack and a line was thrown from it to the most advanced of the party, who was balancing himself among the heaving bergs. This line was made fast to a light skin boat that the party had pushed out over the ice from the shore, and, getting into it, they soon managed to get themselves fairly launched and free from the tossing, wave-dashed ice which momentarily threatened to engulf them.

Mr. Herring, the officer in charge, reported that they had proceeded along the coast as far as Cape Wankarem and had been so fortunate as to accomplish the main objects of their mission, namely, to determine the value of the stories prevalent among the natives to the southward of here concerning the lost whalers Vigilant and Mount Wollaston; to ascertain whether any of the crews of the missing vessels had landed on the Siberian coast to the southeastward of Cape Yakán; and in case any party should land there in the future, to bespeak in their behalf the aid and good-will of the natives.

[73]

The Cruise of the Corwin

At the Chukchi village at Cape Onman they were told that at the village of Oncarima, near Cape Wankarem, they would find three men who could tell them all about the broken ship, for they had seen the wreck and been aboard of her, and had brought off many things that they had found on the deck and in the cabin. This news caused them to hurry on, and when they arrived at the village, and had bestowed the customary presents of tobacco and coffee, Mr. Herring stated the object of his visit.

Three natives then came forward and stated through the interpreter that last year, when they were out hunting seals on the ice, about five miles from the land, near the little island which they call Konkarpo, at the time of year when the new ice begins to grow in the sea, and when the sun does not rise, they saw a big ship without masts in the ice-pack, which they reached without difficulty and climbed on deck. The masts, they said, had been chopped down, and there was a pair of horns on the end of the jib-boom, indicating the position of them on a sketch of a ship. The hold, they said, was full of water so that they could not go down into it to see anything, but they broke a way into the cabin and found four dead men, who had been dead a long time. Three of them were lying in bunks, and one on the floor. They also got into the galley and found a number of articles which they brought away; also, some from the cabin and other parts of the ship.

While they were busy looking for things which they fancied, and considered worth carrying away, one of the three called out to his companions that the wind was blowing offshore, and that they must make haste for the land as the ice was beginning to move, which caused them to hurry from the wreck with what articles they could conveniently carry without being delayed. Next day they went as far out towards the spot where they had left the vessel as the state of the ice would allow, hoping to procure something else. But they found that she had drifted out of sight, and as the wind had been blowing from the southwest, they supposed that she had drifted in a northeasterly direction. They had looked for this ship many times after her first disappearance, but never saw her again.

After they had finished their story, Mr. Herring requested them to show him all the things that they had brought from the wreck, telling them that he would give them tobacco for some of them that he might want to show to his friends. Thereupon they brought forward the following articles, which were carefully examined by our party in hopes of being able to identify the vessel:—

A pair of marine glasses
A pair of silver-mounted spectacles in a tin case (the lenses showing that they had belonged to an aged person)
A jack-knife
A carving-knife
A butcher's chopping-knife
Two table-knives, the handle of one of them marked V
A meat saw
A soup ladle
A stew pan
A tin collander
A hand lamp
A square tin lantern painted green
A draw-knife
An adze
Two carpenter's saws

A chisel
A file
A brace and bit
A tack hammer
A pump-handle
A shovel
A bullet-mould
A truss
A bottle of some sort of medicine
A sailor's ditty bag, with thread
A razor
A linen jumper
Two small coins
Two coils of Manila rope
Three whale spades
One harpoon

The harpoon and whale spades are marked "B.K.," and will no doubt serve to identify the owners. Not a single private name was found on any of the articles; nor did the natives produce any books or papers of any sort, though they said that they saw books in the cabin. A number of the articles enumerated above were purchased by Mr. Herring and are now on board the Corwin, namely, the marine glasses, spectacles, harpoon, and table-knives.

The fate, then, of one of the two missing ships is discovered beyond a doubt, though a portion of the crew may possibly be alive. If the statement as to the deer horns on the jib-boom is to be relied on, it is the Vigilant, as she is said to be the only vessel in the fleet that had deer horns on her jib-boom.

Return of the Search Party

A party of Chukchi traders, also, were met here, being on their way to East Cape with reindeer skins. They stated that no vessel had been seen anywhere along the coast to the northwest of Wankarem as far as Cape Yakán except one, a three-masted steamer, the Vega, two years ago; that if any ships had been seen they certainly should have heard about it. The place where the Vega wintered,[1] fifteen or twenty miles to the northwest of Cape Serdzekamen, is well known to nearly all the natives living within a hundred miles of it.

The Jeannette was last seen by the natives off Cape Serdzek-amen two years ago, probably just before she went north into the ice. A party of walrus hunters went aboard of her. They described her as a three-masted steamer, with plenty of coal and dogs on deck. When Wrangell Land was pointed out on a chart to the natives at Camp Wankarem, they shook their heads and said that they knew nothing of land in that direction. But one old man told them that long ago he had heard something about a party of men who had come from some far unknown land to the north, over the ice.

According to Lieutenant Reynolds, nine Chukchi settlements were passed on the coast between Tapkan and Oncarima, namely, Naskan, Undrillan, Illwinoop, Youngilla,[2] Illoiuk, Koliuchin, Unatapkan, Onman, and Enelpan. The largest of these is Koliuchin, with twenty-seven houses and about three hundred people.

The natives, everywhere along the route traveled, treated the party with great kindness, giving them food for their dog-teams and

[1]Pittle Keg.
[2]Iintlin.

[77]

answering the questions put to them with good-natured patience. At Koliuchin one of the chief men of the village invited them to dinner and greatly surprised them by giving them good tea served in handsome China cups, which he said he had bought from the Russians.

9

Villages of the Dead

STEAMER CORWIN, EAST CAPE, SIBERIA, JULY 1, 1881   After getting our search party on board at Tapkan, we found it impossible, under the conditions of ice and water that prevailed, to land our Chukchi dog-driver, who lives there, and who had come off with the party to get his pay. He was in excellent spirits, however, and told the Captain that since he had received a gun and a liberal supply of ammunition he did not care where he was put ashore— Cape Serdzekamen, East Cape, or any point along the shore or edge of the ice-pack would answer, as he could kill plenty of birds and seals, and get home any time. The dogs and sledges were left in his care at Tapkan, to be in readiness in case they should be required next winter.

Speeding southward under steam and sail we reached East Cape yesterday at seven in the morning. By this time the wind was blowing what seamen call a "living gale," whitening the sea, and filling up the air with blinding scud. We found good anchorage, however, back of the high portion of the Cape, opposite a large settlement of Chukchis. East Cape is a very bold bluff of granite about two thousand feet high, which evidently has been overswept from the northwest. I eagerly waited to get off and to climb high enough to make sure of the trends of the ridges and grooves, and to seek scratches, bossed surfaces, etc. But the howling, shrieking norther blew all day, and had not abated at eleven o'clock last night.

The Cruise of the Corwin

This morning Mr. Nelson and I went ashore to see what we could learn. The village here, through which we passed on our way up the mountain-side, consists of about fifty huts, built on a small, rocky, terminal moraine, and so deeply sunk in the face of the hill that the entire village makes scarcely more show at a distance of a few hundred yards than a group of marmot burrows. The lower portion of the walls is built of moraine boulders, the upper portion and the curving beehive roof of driftwood and the ribs of whales, framed together and covered with walrus hide or dirt.

During the winter the huts are entered by a low tunnel, so as to exclude the cold air as much as possible. The floor is simply the natural dirt mixed into a dark hairy paste, with much that is not at all natural. Fires are made occasionally in the middle of the floor to cook the small portion of their food that is not eaten raw. Ivory-headed spears, arrows, seal nets, bags of oil, rags of seal or walrus meat, and strips of whale blubber and skin, lie on shelves or hang confusedly from the roof, while puppies and nursing mother-dogs and children may be seen scattered here and there, or curled snugly in the pots and eating-troughs, after they have licked them clean, making a kind of squalor that is picturesque and daring beyond conception.

In all of the huts, however, there are from one to three or four luxurious bedrooms. The walls, ceiling, and floor are of soft rein-deer skins, and [each polog has] a trough filled with oil for heat and light. After hunting all day on the ice, making long, rough, stormy journeys, the Chukchi hunter, muffled and hungry, comes into his burrow, eats his fill of oil and seal or walrus meat, then strips himself naked and lies down in his closed fur nest, his polog, in glorious ease, to smoke and sleep.

I was anxious to reach the top of the cape peninsula to learn surely whether it had been overswept by an ice-sheet, and if so from what direction, and to study its glacial conditions in general and the character of the rocks. I therefore hastened to make the most of my opportunity, and pushed on through the village towards the lowest part of the divide between the north and south sides, followed by a crowd of curious boys, who good-naturedly assisted me whenever I stopped to gather the flowers that I found in bloom. The banks of a stream coming from a high basin filled with snow was quite richly flowered with anemones, buttercups, potentillas, drabas, primulas, and many species of dwarf willows, up to a height of about a thousand feet above the level of the sea; beyond this, spring had hardly made any impression, while nearly a thousand feet of the highest summits were still covered with deep snow.

Mr. Nelson soon left me in pursuit of a bird, and in crossing a rocky ridge to come up with me again, he came upon a lot of other game, which seemed to interest him still more, namely, dead natives scattered about on the rough stones at one of the cemeteries belonging to the village. The bodies of the dead, together with whatever articles belonged to them, are simply laid on the surface of the ground, so that a cemetery is a good field for collectors. A lot of ivory spears, arrows, dishes of various kinds, and a stone hammer, formed the least ghastly of his spoils. Leaving Mr. Nelson alone in his glory, I pushed on to the top of the divide, then followed it westward to the highest summit on the peninsula, whence I obtained the views I was in search of.

The dividing ridge all along the high eastern portion of the peninsula is rounded from nearly north to south. The curves on the north begin almost at the waters' edge, while the south side is quite precipitous along the shore. There is also a telling series of parallel grooves and ridges trending north and south across the peninsula. The highest point is about twenty-five hundred feet above the sea, and the mountainous portion has been nearly eroded from the continent and made an island like the two Diomedes, the wide gap of low ground connecting it with the high mainland being only a few feet above tide-water. In this low portion there is here and there a rounded upswelling of more resisting rock, with trends, all telling the same story of a vast oversweeping ice-flood from the north.

I also had a clear view of the coast mountains for a hundred miles or thereabouts, all of which are tellingly glaciated in harmony with the above generalization. Most of the rock is granite with cleavage planes that cause it to weather rapidly into flat blocks. One conical black hill, fifteen hundred feet high, is volcanic rock, close-grained and dense like some kinds of iron ore. I saw an Arctic owl, a big snowy fellow, fitting his place; also, snow-buntings and linnets. When the natives saw Mr. Nelson returning without me they said that he had killed me, not being aware of the fact that he understood their language.

On my way down to the shore I crossed another of the village cemeteries on a very rough and steep slope of weathered granite, several hundred feet above the village and to the westward of it. Whole skeletons or single bones and skulls lay here and there, wedged into chance positions among the stones, weathering and falling to pieces like the ivory-pointed spears, arrows, etc., mixed with them. The mountain that they were lying on is crumbling also—dust to dust. Some of the corpses have had stones piled on them, and their goods on top of all; others were laid on the rough rocks with a row of big stones on the lower side to keep them from rolling down.

Villages of the Dead

The damp, lower portion of the wild north wind, as it was deflected up and over the slopes and frosty summit of the peninsula, has given birth to a remarkably beautiful covering of white ice crystals on the windward sides of exposed boulders, and in some places on the snow. The crystals resemble white feathers in their aggregate forms, but are firm and icy in structure, and as evenly and gracefully imbricated on each other over the rough faces of the rocks as are the feathers on the breast of a bird. The effect is marvelously beautiful and interesting as seen on those castellated rock-piles, so frequently found on bleak summits. The points of the feathers grow to windward, and indicate by their curves all the varying directions pursued by the interrupted wind as it glints and reverberates about the innumerable angles of the rock fronts. Thus the rocks, where the exposure to storms is greatest, and where only ruin seems to be the object, are all the more lavishly clothed upon with beauty—beauty that grows with and depends upon the violence of the gale. In like manner do men find themselves enriched by storms that seem only big with ruin, both in the physical and the moral worlds.

We weighed anchor and got away at two o'clock in the afternoon and reached the West Diomede Island village at half-past four. Here we took aboard the boatswain and Mr. Nelson's man, whom we had left to make observations on the currents, tides, etc. He was to have been assisted by the natives, but the rough weather prevented work. About half-past five we left the Diomede for Marcus Bay in order to land Joe, the Chukchi. The sea is smooth now, at a quarter of an hour before midnight, and there is a lovely orange-and-gold sunset. The gulls are still on the wing.

JULY 2   Clear, calm, sunful; the coast of Asia is seen to excellent advantage; crowds of glacial peaks, ice-fountains, and fiords far inreaching. The snow on them is melting fast. About noon[1] twelve canoes from a large village twenty miles north of Marcus Bay came off to trade. The schooners that came to this region to trade were perhaps afraid to touch here. Consequently the Corwin was the first vessel with trade goods that they have seen this year, and the business in bone and ivory went on with hearty vigor. A hundred or more Chukchis were aboard at once, making a stir equal to that of a country fair. One of them spoke a little whaler English, three quarters of which was profanity and nearly one quarter slang. He asked the Captain why he did not like him, [and intimated that] if he should come ashore to his house he, the Indian, would show him by his treatment that he liked him very much.

We are now, at five in the afternoon, approaching Marcus Bay, where Joe lives, for the purpose of taking him home. For his month's work and his team of five dogs he has been paid a box of hard bread, ten sacks of flour, some calico, a rifle, and a considerable quantity of ammunition. Although this is doubtless five times more than he expected, he does not show any excitement or rise of spirits, but only a stoical composure, which seems so Arctic and immovable that I doubt whether he would move a muscle of his face if he were presented with the whole ship's cargo and the ship itself thrown in.

STEAMER CORWIN, ST. LAWRENCE ISLAND, ALASKA, JULY 3, 1881   St. Lawrence Island, the largest in Bering Sea, is situated at a distance of about one hundred and twenty miles off the mouths

[1]Opposite Cape Chaplin.

of the Yukon, and forty-five miles from the nearest point on the coast of Siberia. It is about a hundred miles in length from east to west and fifteen miles in average width; a dreary, cheerless-looking mass of black lava, dotted with volcanoes, covered with snow, without a single tree, and rigidly bound in ocean ice for more than half the year.

Inasmuch as it lies broadsidewise to the way pursued by the great ice-sheet that once filled Bering Sea, it is traversed by numerous valleys and ridges and low gaps, some of which have been worn down nearly to the sea-level. Had the glaciation to which it has been subjected been carried on much longer, then, instead of this one large island, we should have had several smaller ones. Nearly all of the volcanic cones with which the central portion of the island is in great part covered are post-glacial in age and present well-formed craters but little weathered as yet.

All the surface of the low grounds, in the glacial gaps, as well as the flat table-lands is covered with wet, spongy tundra of mosses and lichens, with patches of blooming heathworts and dwarf willows, and grasses and sedges, diversified here and there by drier spots, planted with larkspurs, saxifrages, daisies, primulas, anemones, ferns, etc. These form gardens with a luxuriance and brightness of color little to be hoped for in so cold and dreary-looking a region.

Three years ago there were about fifteen hundred inhabitants on the island, chiefly Eskimos, living in ten villages located around the shores, and subsisting on the seals, walruses, whales, and water birds that abound here. Now there are only about five hundred people, most of them in one village on the northwest end of the island, nearly two thirds of the population having died of starvation during the winter of 1878–79. In seven of the villages not a single soul was left alive. In the largest village at the northwest end of the island, which suffered least, two hundred out of six hundred died. In the one at the southwest end only fifteen out of about two hundred survived. There are a few survivors also at one of the villages on the east end of the island.

After landing our interpreter at Marcus Bay we steered for St. Michael, and in passing along the north side of this island we stopped an hour or so this morning at one of the smallest of the dead villages. Mr. Nelson went ashore and obtained a lot of skulls and specimens of one sort and another for the Smithsonian Institution. Twenty-five skeletons were seen.

A few miles farther on we anchored before a larger village, situated about halfway between the east and west ends of the island, which I visited in company with Mr. Nelson, the Captain, and the Surgeon. We found twelve desolate huts close to the beach with about two hundred skeletons in them or strewn about on the rocks and rubbish heaps within a few yards of the doors. The scene was indescribably ghastly and desolate, though laid in a country purified by frost as by fire. Gulls, plovers, and ducks were swimming and flying about in happy life, the pure salt sea was dashing white against the shore, the blooming tundra swept back to the snow-clad volcanoes, and the wide azure sky bent kindly over all—nature intensely fresh and sweet, the village lying in the foulest and most glaring death. The shrunken bodies, with rotting furs on them, or white, bleaching skeletons, picked bare by the crows, were lying mixed with kitchen-midden rubbish where they had been cast out by surviving relatives while they yet had strength to carry them.

In the huts those who had been the last to perish were found in bed, lying evenly side by side, beneath their rotting deerskins. A grinning skull might be seen looking out here and there, and a pile of skeletons in a corner, laid there no doubt when no one was left strong enough to carry them through the narrow underground passage to the door. Thirty were found in one house, about half of them piled like fire-wood in a corner, the other half in bed, seeming as if they had met their fate with tranquil apathy. Evidently these people did not suffer from cold, however rigorous the winter may have been, as some of the huts had in them piles of deerskins that had not been in use. Nor, although their survivors and neighbors all say that hunger was the sole cause of their death, could they have battled with famine to the bitter end, because a considerable amount of walrus rawhide and skins of other animals was found in the huts. These would have sustained life at least a week or two longer.

The facts all tend to show that the winter of 1878–79 was, from whatever cause, one of great scarcity, and as these people never lay up any considerable supply of food from one season to another, they began to perish. The first to succumb were carried out of the huts to the ordinary ground for the dead, about half a mile from the village. Then, as the survivors became weaker, they carried the dead a shorter distance, and made no effort to mark their positions or to lay their effects beside them, as they customarily do. At length the bodies were only dragged to the doors of the huts, or laid in a corner, and the last survivors lay down in despair without making any struggle to prolong their wretched lives by eating the last scraps of skin.

Mr. Nelson went into this Golgotha with hearty enthusiasm, gathering the fine white harvest of skulls spread before him, and throwing them in heaps like a boy gathering pumpkins. He brought nearly a hundred on board, which will be shipped with specimens of bone armor, weapons, utensils, etc., on the Alaska Commercial Company's steamer St. Paul.

We also landed at the village on the southwest corner of the island and interviewed the fifteen survivors. When we inquired where the other people of the village were, one of the group, who speaks a few words of English, answered with a happy, heedless smile, "All mucky." "All gone!" "Dead?" "Yes, dead, all dead!" Then he led us a few yards back of his hut and pointed to twelve or fourteen skeletons lying on the brown grass, repeating in almost a merry tone of voice, "Dead, yes, all dead, all mucky, all gone!"

About two hundred perished here, and unless some aid be extended by our government which claims these people, in a few years at most every soul of them will have vanished from the face of the earth; for, even where alcohol is left out of the count, the few articles of food, clothing, guns, etc., furnished by the traders, exert a degrading influence, making them less self-reliant, and less skillful as hunters. They seem easily susceptible of civilization, and well deserve the attention of our government.

10

Glimpses of Alaskan Tundra

St. michael, alaska, july 8, 1881   The Corwin arrived here on the Fourth, and, in honor of the day, made some noise with her cannon in concert with those belonging to the fort, to the steamer St. Paul, and to the post of the Western Fur and Trading Company across the bay. We have taken on a supply of coal and provisions for nine months, in case we should by any accident be caught in the ice north of Bering Strait before calling here again in the fall.

We hope to get away from here this evening for the Arctic, intending to cruise along the Alaskan coast beyond Point Barrow, spending some time about Kotzebue Sound in order to look after revenue interests, and to make, perhaps, some explorations on the lower courses of the Inland[1] and Buckland Rivers, and on the Colville,[2] of which nearly nothing is yet known to geographers. The coast will also be carefully searched for traces of the Jeannette and missing whalers in case any portion of their crews have come over the ice last winter. Perhaps a month will be spent thus, when an attempt will be made to reach Wrangell Land, where the Jeannette probably spent her first winter. And since the Corwin has already passed Cape Serdzekamen twice this season, we have sanguine hopes of success under so favorable a condition of the ice.

[1]Now called Noatak River.
[2]The upper reaches of the Colville and Buckland Rivers, according to the Geological Survey map of 1915, are still unexplored. The former empties into the Arctic Ocean, the latter into Eschscholtz Bay.

The Cruise of the Corwin

Arctic explorations are exciting much interest among the natives here. Last evening the shamans called up the spirits supposed to be familiar with polar matters. The latter informed them that not only was the Jeannette forever lost in the ice of the Far North with all her crew, but also that the Corwin would never more be seen after leaving St. Michael this time, information which caused our interpreter to leave us, nor have we as yet been able to procure another in his place. The Jeannette took two men from here.[1]

This is the busy time of the year at St. Michael, when the traders come with their furs from stations far up the Yukon and return with next year's supply of goods. Those of the Western Fur and Trading Company left for the upper Yukon yesterday, and those connected with the Alaska Commercial Company will follow as soon as the new steamboat, which they are putting together here, can be got ready.

The party of prospectors which left San Francisco this spring in a schooner, to seek a mountain of solid silver, reported to have been seen some distance up a river that flows into Golofnin Bay on the north side of Norton Sound, about one hundred miles from here, has arrived, and is now up the river prospecting. From what I can learn, they will not find the mountain to be solid silver, but some far commoner mineral. Gold is said to have been discovered by Mr. Harker on the Tanana River—bar diggings that would pay about twelve dollars per day. There will probably be a rush to the new mines ere long, though news of this kind is kept back as long as possible by the fur companies.

[1] These were the two native Alaskan hunters Alexey and Aneguin. The former was among those who perished with De Long on the delta of the Lena River.

Glimpses of Alaskan Tundra

The weather is delightful, temperature about 60° F. in the shade, and the vegetation is growing with marvelous rapidity. The grass already is about two feet high about the shores of the bay, making a bright green surface, not at all broken as far as can be seen from the steamer. Almost any number of cattle would find excellent pasturage here for three or four months in the year.

During our last visit Dr. Rosse and I crossed the tundra to a prominent hill about seven miles to the southward from the redoubt. We found the hill to be a well-formed volcanic cone with a crater a hundred yards in diameter and about twenty feet deep, from the rim of which I counted upwards of forty others within a distance of thirty or forty miles. This old volcano is said by the medicine men to be the entrance to the spirit world for their tribe, and the rumbling sounds heard occasionally are supposed to be caused by the spirits when they are conducting in a dead Indian. The last eruption was of ashes and pumice cinders, which are strewn plentifully around the rim of the crater and down the sides of the cone.

Our walk was very fatiguing, as we sank deep in spongy moss at every step, and staggered awkwardly on the tops of tussocks of grass and sedge, which bent and let our feet down between them. It was very delightful, however, and crowded with rare beauty.

We saw a great number of birds, most of which were busy about their nests; there were ptarmigan, snipes, curlews, sandpipers, song sparrows, titmice, loons, many species of ducks, and the Emperor goose. The ptarmigan is a magnificent bird, about the size of the dusky grouse of the Sierra. They are quite abundant here, flying up with a vigorous whirr of wings and a loud, hearty, cackling "kek-kek-kep" every few yards all the way across the tun-

dra. The cocks frequently took up a position on some slight emi-
nence to observe us. They seemed happily in place out on the wide
moor, with abundance of berries to eat through the summer,
spring, and fall, and willows and alder buds for winter. Then they
are pure white, and warmly feathered down to the ends of their
toes. The sandpipers had fine feeding-grounds about the shallow
pools. The gray moor is a fine place for curlews, too, and snipe.

The plants in bloom were primula, andromeda, dicentra,
mertensia, veratrum, ledum, saxifrage, empetrum, cranberry,
draba of several species, lupine, stellaria, silene, polemonium,
buckbean, bryanthus, several sedges, a liliaceous plant new to me,
five species of willow, dwarf birch, alder, and a purple pedicularis,
the showiest of them all. The primula and a bryanthus-like heathwort were the most beautiful.

The tundra is composed of a close sponge of mosses about a
foot deep, with lichens growing on top of the mosses, and a thin
growth of grasses and sedges and most of the flowering plants mentioned above, with others not then in bloom. The moss rests upon
a stratum of solid ice, and the ice on black vesicular lava, ridges of
which rise here and there above the spongy mantle of moss, and
afford ground for plants that like a dry soil. There are hollows, too,
beneath the general level along which grow tall aspidiums, grasses,
sedges, larkspurs, alders, and willows—the alders five or six inches
in diameter and from eight to ten feet high, the largest timber I
have seen since leaving California.

Visits from Indians in kayaks. At full speed they can run about
seven miles an hour for a short distance. The salmon, that is, the
best red-fleshed species, are about finishing their run up the river
now. A very fat one, weighing about fifty pounds, was bought from
an Indian for a little hardtack. After enough had been cut from it

for one meal, it was lost overboard by dropping from its head while suspended by it. Specimens of a hundred pounds or more are said to be caught at times. Mr. Nelson saw dried specimens six feet long.

[STEAMER CORWIN, EN ROUTE TO THE ARCTIC OCEAN.] JULY 9   Left St. Michael, having on board provisions for nine months, and about one hundred tons of coal. Decks heavily piled. A weird red sunset; land miraged into most grotesque forms. Heavy smoke from the burning tundra southwest from St. Michael. The season's cruise seems now to be just beginning.

JULY 10   Arrived this morning, about seven o'clock, in Golofnin Bay, and dropped anchor. There is a heavy sea and a stiff south wind, with clouds veiling the summits down to a thousand feet from sea level. I was put ashore on the right side of the bay after breakfast at a small Indian village of two huts made of driftwood. They were full of dried herring. Inhabitants not at home, but saw a few at another village farther up the bay. All the huts are strictly conical and of driftwood. A few Indians came off in canoes, very fine ones, of a slightly different pattern from any others I have seen. There is a round hole through the front end to facilitate lifting. I had a long walk and returned to the ship at three in the afternoon.

The principal fact I discovered is a heavy deposit of glacial drift about fifty feet high, facing several miles of coast. It is coarsely stratified and water-worn—the material of a terminal moraine, leveled by water flowing from a broad glacier, while separated from the sea by a low, draggled flat, and then eaten into bluffs by the sea waves. It is now overgrown with alders, willows, and a good crop of sedges and grasses, bright with flowers.[1] Found the small blue vi-

[1]See "Botanical Notes," p. 265.

olet rather common. White spiræa, in flower, is abundant in damp places about alder groves where the tundra mosses are not too thick. The cranberries, huckleberries, and rubus will soon be ripe. The purple-flowered rubus is only in bloom now.

The driftwood is spruce and cottonwood. The rock, containing mica, slate, and a good deal of quartz, seems favorable for gold. The life-boat, rigged with sails, has been sent to board the prospectors' schooner anchored farther up the bay. Seven men are aboard, and seven are off prospecting. They are reported to have found promising galena assaying high values per ton. They mean to visit the quicksilver mines on the Kuskoquim. The rocks on the opposite side of the bay exhibit clear traces of glacial sculpture.

JULY 11   Sailed this morning from the anchorage in Golofnin Bay, and reached Sledge Island at nine in the evening. The natives are mostly away on the mainland. The island seems to be of granite and to have been overswept [by glaciers]. Obtained a pretty good view of the mountains at the head of Golofnin Bay. They seem to be from four to five thousand feet high.

JULY 12   Reached King Island this morning about seven o'clock, and left at half-past ten. Reached Cape Prince of Wales about three in the afternoon and anchored. Left at six in the evening. Clear, bright day; water, pale green. Had a fine view of the Diomedes, Fairway Rock, King Island, Cape Prince of Wales, and the lofty mountains towards the head of the river that enters Golofnin Bay, all from one point of view. The King Island natives were away on the mainland, all save a few old or crippled men, and women and children.

Their town, of all that I have seen, is the most remarkably situated, on the face of a steep slope, almost a cliff, and presents a very strange appearance. Some fifty stone huts, scarcely visible at a short distance, like those of the Arizona cliff-dwellers, rise like heaps of stones among heaps of stones. These are the winter huts, and are entered by tunnels. The summer huts, large square boxes on stilts, are of skin, [stretched over] large poles of driftwood. There is no way of landing save amid a mass of great wave-beaten boulders. In stormy times the King Islanders' excellent canoes have to be pitched off into the sea when a wave is about to recede. Two are tied together for safety in rough weather. These pairs live in any sea. A few gray-headed old pairs came off with some odds and ends to trade.

Mr. Nelson and I went ashore to obtain photographs and sketches and to bargain for specimens of ivory carvings, etc. A busy trade developed on the roof of a house, the only level ground. Groups of merry boys went skipping nimbly from rock to rock, and busily guided us over the safest places. They showed us where between the huge boulders it was best to attempt a landing, which was difficult. Though the sea was nearly calm, a slight swell made a heavy surf. One hut rose above another like a village on Yosemite walls. The whole island is precipitous, so much so that it seems accessible only to murres, etc., which flock here in countless multitudes to breed.

In the afternoon, at Cape Prince of Wales, we lay opposite a large village whose inhabitants have a bad character. They started a fight while trading on board of a schooner. Many of them were killed, and they have since been distrusted not only on account of their known bad character, but also because of the law of blood revenge which obtains universally among these natives. They are noted traders and go far in their large skin boats which carry sails.

While we were here a canoe, met by our search party, arrived from East Cape—a party of Chukchi traders, bringing deerskins from Cape Yakán. They are in every way much better-looking men than the natives of this side, being taller, better-formed, and more cordial in manner. They at once recognized our Third Lieutenant Reynolds, whom they had met at Tapkan. Fog at night; going under sail only.

JULY 13   Lovely day, nearly cloudless. Average temperature of 50° F. At half-past five in the afternoon we fell in with a trading schooner[1] opposite an Indian village.[2] One of the boats came alongside the Corwin and traded a few articles. Nothing contraband was found, though rifles probably had been sold during the first part of her cruise. These vessels, as well as whalers, carry more or less whiskey and rifles in order to obtain ivory, whalebone, and furs. They go from coast to coast and among islands, and thus pick up valuable cargoes. The natives cannot understand why the Corwin interferes with trade in repeating rifles and whiskey. They consider it all a matter of rivalry and superior strength. No wonder, since our government does nothing for them. Common rifles would be better for them, partly on account of the difficulty of obtaining supplies of cartridges, and partly because repeating rifles tempt them to destroy large amounts of game which they do not need. The reindeer has in this manner been well-nigh exterminated within the last few years.

JULY 14   A hot, sunny day. Came to anchor this morning at the head of Kotzebue Sound opposite the mouth of the Kiwalik

[1]The O. S. Fowler.
[2]Near Cape Espenberg.

Glimpses of Alaskan Tundra

River. Between eight and nine o'clock this morning Lieutenant Reynolds, with six seamen, took Mr. Nelson and me up the river in one of the boats. We reached a point about eight miles from the mouth of the estuary near the head of the delta. Since the bay is shoal off the estuary, the ship was anchored about four miles from the mouth. We, therefore, had a journey of about twenty-four miles altogether. We first landed at the mouth of the estuary and walked a mile or two along a bar shoved up by the waves and the ice. Here we found one native hut in good repair. The inhabitants were away, but the trodden grass showed that they had not been gone very long. This is the time of the year when the grand gathering of the clans for trade takes place at Cape Blossom, and they probably had gone there. The floor of the hut was about ten feet in diameter, [and the hut itself] was made of a frame of driftwood covered with sod, and was entered by a narrow tunnel two feet high and eighteen inches wide. We saw traces of a great many houses, showing that quite a large village was at one time located here. In some only a few decaying timbers were to be seen, in others all the timbers had vanished and only the excavation remained. Some six miles farther up the stream I noticed other ruins, indicating that many natives once lived here, though now their number has dwindled to one family.

The delta is about five miles wide and about eight miles long. It is covered with a grassy, flowery, sedgy vegetation, with pools, lagoons, and branches of the river here and there. It is a lonely place, and a favorite resort of ducks, geese, and other water birds which come here to breed and to moult. We saw swans[1] with their

[1] Whistling swans *(Olor columbianus)*.

young; eider ducks, also, were seen with their young, and some were found on their eggs, which are green and about the size of hens' eggs. Their nests were among the grass on the margin of a lagoon and were made with a handful of down from their breasts. These as well as other ducks, which had their young with them, could not be made to fly, though we came within three or four yards of them in a narrow pool. When I threw sticks at the flock they would only dive. They were very graceful, and took good care of their children. We could easily have killed them all.

The wild geese which we saw also had young—a dozen families altogether.[1] They are moulting now and cannot fly. We chased a large flock in the estuary. When they saw us coming, they made frantic efforts to keep ahead of the boat. When we overtook them, they dived and scattered, coming up here and there, often close to the boat, and always trying to keep themselves concealed by laying their necks along the water and sinking their bodies and lying perfectly still; or, if they were well away from the boat and fancied themselves unseen, they swam in this sunken, outstretched condition and were soon lost to view, if there was the least wind-ripple on the water. Saw three plovers, the godwit from the Siberian side, and many finches and gulls. On a small islet in the middle of a pond we found one nest of the burgomaster gull. They tried to drive us away by swooping down upon us. I noticed also the robber-gull and several others. Butterflies were quite abundant among the blooming meadow vegetation. I noticed six or more species. The

---

[1] Mr. E. W. Nelson reported the geese observed here as belonging to two species, the American white-fronted goose *(Anser albifrons gambeli)* and the white-cheeked goose *(Bernicla canadensis leucoparia)*.

vegetation is like that of Cape Prince of Wales and Norton Sound. Found one red poppy, one wintergreen, allium, saxifrages, primulas, lupines, pedicularis, and peas, quite abundant. This region is noted for its fossil ivory. Found only a fragment of a tusk and a few bones. The deposit whence they were derived is probably above the point reached by us. The gravel is composed of quartz, mica, slate, and lava. There are many lava cones and ridges on both sides of the estuary.

11

Caribou and a Native Fair

JULY 15   Rainy and cold; cleared at seven in the evening. Left the head of Kotzebue Sound this morning at seven-thirty, for Cape Blossom, where the natives assemble from near and far to trade, but only one poor family was left. We went ashore and found them engaged in fishing for salmon with a net which was pushed out from the shore by a long pole sixty feet in length, made of three tied together. The Indians had gone fifteen or twenty miles up the coast, near Cape Krusenstern. Their tents were to be seen, looking like Oakland across the bay from San Francisco, so numerous they seemed. A small schooner, the Fowler, was at anchor there trading. Soon half a dozen canoes came alongside of us, and offered to trade, but asked big prices. The Captain obtained only two wolf-skins, a deerskin, and a few muskrats, and bunches of sinew. [The Corwin then proceeded to Hotham Inlet and came to anchor about two miles from the native village called Sheshalek, inhabited by Kobuk and Noatak River Eskimos.]

JULY 16   A fresh breeze from the north, but the day is tolerably clear. A swell is breaking into whitecaps here and there. A busy day with the Indians, trading for a winter supply of deerskins. We obtained over a hundred altogether at the rate of about a dollar each for summer skins, and half as much for those taken in winter. With what we have already picked up here and there, and with the parkas we have collected, this will be amply sufficient. Reindeer are killed in immense numbers inland from here. All are wild; no domesticated herds are found on the American continent, though the natives have illustrations enough of their value on the opposite shores of Bering Sea. These Indians prefer herds that require no care, though they are not always to be found when wanted. Some of the wild herds that exist up the Inland River are said, by the Indians, to be so large as to require more than a day in passing.

The number of these animals, considering the multitude of their enemies, is truly wonderful. The large gray wolves kill many during the winter, and when the snow is deep, large flocks are slaughtered by the Indians, whether they need them or not. They make it a rule to kill every animal that comes within reach, without a thought of future scarcity, fearing, as some say, that, should they refuse to kill as opportunity offers, though it be at a time when food is no object, then the deer-spirit would be offended at the refusal of his gifts and would not send any deer when they are in want. Probably, however, they are moved simply by an instinctive love of killing on which their existence depends, and these wholesale slaughters are to be regarded as only too much of a good thing. Formerly there were large herds about St. Michael, but since the introduction of repeating rifles they have wholly vanished. Hundreds were surrounded in passes among the hills, were killed and left lying where they fell, not even the hides being taken. Often a band of moose or reindeer is overtaken in deep snow, when they are easily killed with clubs by Indians on snowshoes, who will simply cut out their tongues, and leave the rest to be eaten by wolves.

The reindeer is found throughout the Arctic and subarctic regions of both Asia and America, and, in either the wild or the domestic state, supplies to the natives an abundance of food and warm clothing, thus rendering these bleak and intensely cold regions inhabitable. I believe it is only in Lapland and Siberia that the reindeer is domesticated. They are never sold alive by the Chukchis on account of a superstitious notion that to do so would surely bring bad luck by incensing the spirit of the deer. A hundred can be bought, after they are killed, for less than one alive. Certain ceremonies must also be observed before killing.

Out on the frozen tundra great care is required, both by day and by night, to keep them from being scattered and torn by wolves. A reindeer weighs from three to four hundred pounds. The winter skins are heavier, the hair being long and tipped with white, giving them a hoary appearance, especially on the back; but the hair is easily broken and pulled out, a fact which renders them much less durable when used for bedding, tents, or clothing than those taken in summer, when the hair is short, and dark blue, almost black. Reindeer hides are easily tanned; those tanned in Siberia are dyed a rich reddish-brown on the inside with alder bark. The domestic reindeer skins are considered better than those of the wild animals. Wrangell[1] has described the herds as affording a grand sight.

At this point[2] the Indians from the interior, and from many miles up and down the coast, assemble once a year in July to trade with each other, with parties of Chukchis who come from Siberia in umiaks, and with the few schooners that bring goods from San Francisco and from the Sandwich Islands. After trading they indulge in games of wrestling, playing ball, gambling, dancing, and

[1]Admiral Baron Ferdinand Petrovich von Wrangell, polar explorer and Russian Governor, Administrator of the Russian-American colonies, 1829–36.
[2]The head of Kotzebue Sound.

drinking whiskey, if they can get it. Then they break up their camps and go to their widely scattered homes, some a month's journey or more up the Inland and down the Colville Rivers. They now have about one hundred and forty tents set in a row along the beach, their light kayaks in front of the tents in a neat row, each with paddles and spears that belong to it, and in front of these a row of large skin umiaks. They are a mixed, jolly multitude, wearing different ornaments, superb fur clothes, or shabby foreign articles; one sees long hair, short hair, or closely shaven; here is headgear of hats, caps, or cowls, and folk who go bareheaded; labrets, too, of every conceivable size, color, and material—glass, stone, beads, ivory, brass. They show good taste and ingenuity in the manufacture of pipes, weapons, knickknacks of a domestic kind, utensils, ornaments, boats, etc.

Though savage and sensual, they are by no means dull or apathetic like the sensual savages of civilization, who live only to eat and indulge the senses, for these Eskimos, without newspapers or telegraphs, know all that is going on within hundreds of miles, and are keen questioners and alive to everything that goes on before them. They dearly like to gossip. One tried to buy some of the cabin boy's hair, on account of its curious whiteness; another, who has red hair, is followed and commented on with ludicrous interest.

The shores hereabouts are comparatively low, the hills, back a few miles from shore, rolling and of moderate height, and mountains are to be seen beyond.

JULY 17   The northerly wind still prevails; cloudy all day, but dry. Left the Eskimo "Long Branch" at four o'clock in the morning and sailed to Cape Thompson, where we mean to look into the condition of the Eskimos and inquire whether they have obtained whiskey from any of the traders, contrary to law. The coast is rather low. Mountains are visible thirty miles back; low hills between.

JULY 18   Numerous snow squalls. Came to anchor at five this morning in the lee of Point Hope. Norther blowing. Remained all day in company with the Sea Breeze.[1] A few of the natives came off shore—good-natured fellows. A negro, who wintered here last season, was well used by them, for he was given the best of what they had. He had lost an axe overboard, so the story goes, and deserted on account of trouble he had over the matter with the second officer of the brig Hidalgo. He was taken on board again this spring.

We landed and walked through the village. Found a fine gravel beach, beautifully flowered beyond the reach of the waves. Most of the natives seem to be away—at the summer gathering, perhaps. The graveyard is of great extent and very conspicuous from the custom of surrounding the graves with poles.

JULY 19   Cold, stiff, north wind; clear. Left our anchorage at five o'clock this morning and proceeded north, but found the gale too strong to make much headway and, therefore, turned back and anchored at Cape Thompson, thirty miles south of Point Hope. Watering ship all day; the wind is blowing hard. Going north again since seven o'clock this evening. Wind moderating slightly.

I went ashore this forenoon and, after passing a few minutes interviewing a group of vagabond natives from Point Hope who

[1]A whaling bark.

were camped here to gather eggs, kill murres, and loaf, I pushed on up the hillside, whose sheer scarped face forms the Cape. I found it five hundred and fifty feet high, composed of calcareous slates, much bent and contorted, and a considerable portion was fossiliferous. Where hills of this rock have steep slopes, and so much drainage and wash that soil is not allowed to form, nor the usual moss mantle to grow, they bleach white and present a remarkably desolate aspect in the distance. Such hills are common back of Kotzebue Sound. These barren slopes, however, alternate with remarkably fertile valleys, where flowers of fifty or more species bloom in rich profusion, making masses of white, purple, and blue. Sometimes this occurs on a comparatively thin soil where the leaves do not veil the rocky ground; but at the bottom of the valleys there usually is a green ground below the bloom.

The slopes over which I passed in to-day's walk are planted chiefly with sweet fern—Dryas—with its yellowish-white flowers. A purple silene is also very abundant, making beautiful bosses of color. Phlox is present in dwarfed masses, only the stems and leaves being dwarfed, not the flowers. Anemones occur in fine patches, and buttercups, and several species of daisies and lupines. Dodecatheon I met here for the first time this season. Dwarf willows are abundant. There was one fern and one heathwort along a streamside. I saw no true tundra here, its absence, no doubt, being due to the free drainage of the surface. The winds from the north are violent here, as evidenced by the immense snow-drifts still unmelted along the shore where we landed, and also back in the hollows where they feed the stream at which we got water for the ship. They probably will last all summer. This circumstance, of course, leaves the hill slopes all the barer and dryer.

The Cruise of the Corwin

The trends of two main ridges, of which I obtained approximate measurements, probably coincide with the direction of the movement of the ice. There is a small wasted moraine in the lower part of the stream valley, extending to the shore. Partial afterglaciation has been light, and on rocks of this sort has left only very faint traces.

JULY 20 Last night we again anchored on the south side of Point Hope, the norther still blowing hard. About noon to-day it began to abate, and we again pushed off northward. Now, at eight o'clock in the evening, we are approaching Cape Lisburne, a bold bluff of gray stratified rocks about fifteen hundred feet high. All along the coast, from the neighborhood of Cape Prince of Wales, the peculiar gray color of the rocks, and the forms into which they are weathered and glaciated, indicate one continuous formation, partially described yesterday. Magnificent sections are exposed between the north side of Point Hope and Cape Lisburne. The age of the formation I do not as yet certainly know. The existence of coal-veins here and there in connection with conglomerates, and the few fossils, would tend to identify it as Carboniferous, though some of the sections show a wide vertical range. Probably a considerable amount of the formation is older. The few fossils I have seen point to the Carboniferous, or older formations.

Between eleven and twelve o'clock this forenoon several white whales were seen near the shore, showing their white backs above the water when they rose to breathe, so white at a little distance that they might easily have been mistaken for breaking waves. We saw the Indians shoot and kill one, and went ashore to have a good look at this Beluga. It proved to be a small one, only about seven feet long, and of a pale gray ashen color, probably a young specimen. In general form it is like a whale, but more slender. The head is narrow and rather high in the forehead. The eyes are very small, about five eighths of an inch in diameter. The ears are hardly visible, would scarcely admit a common lead pencil. The blow-hole, as in the true whales, is about an inch in diameter. The forefeet, the only limbs, are in the form of short flippers, and the tail, which is large, is formed by an expansion of the thick skin. They are more nearly related to the dolphins than to the whales—the dolphins, porpoises, and grampuses forming one of the divisions of the three *Cetacea delphinoidea*.

While we were ashore looking at this specimen, a much larger one came along parallel with the shore-line and not more than twenty or thirty yards from it. The natives were on the watch and shot it through the body when it rose to blow. Instead of making out to sea when wounded, it kept its course alongshore and the natives followed excitedly, ready to get another shot. They kept it in sight while it was ten or twelve feet under water, which they were enabled to do on account of its whiteness. Eight or ten men jumped into a canoe and followed it, one standing in the bow with a spear. After swimming about half a mile and receiving four or more bullets from Henry and Winchester rifles, it began to struggle and die. The boat came up, an Eskimo drove in a spear, and the whale was taken in tow and brought back to where the first was killed, the crew, meanwhile, singing in triumph. Then a rolling hitch was made, and a dozen willing hands landed the animal, a female. She measured about twelve feet in length and nine in circumference. They at once began to eat the tail and back fin raw, cutting off blocks of it and giving it to the children, not because they were hungry, but because they regarded it as so very palatable.

Then a fire was built of driftwood. Looking back from the ship, only two red spots were visible on the beach—and a group of fifty feasting Eskimos! Probably not a bit of the Belugas, except a little of the blubber, will be left by night.

The attitudes of the riflemen, legs spread, rifle to shoulder, and eyes vividly on the alert, as they watched the animal's appearance above water, were very striking. These animals are quite abundant hereabouts, and used to be killed with spears that had heads made of stone or ivory. Whales were killed in the same manner. A much larger number of right whales is killed by the natives about the shores of Bering Sea and along the polar shores than is supposed. Almost every village gets from one to five every season. Then comes a joyful time. The bone belongs to the boat's crew that strikes the whale, the carcass to all the village

A mountain slope just to the northeast of Cape Lisburne is so covered at the top with slender, spirey columns of rock, that I at first glance took them for trees. A slight dusting of snow has lately whitened the peaks. To the south of the Cape twelve or fifteen miles two small valleys, cut nearly to the level of the sea, exhibit terminal and lateral moraines. After-glaciation has been light. The higher mountains do not approach the coast nearly. No deep fiords like those of the west coast.

12

Zigzags among the Polar Pack

JULY 21   Rainy this forenoon, clear at night. Wind blowing hard from the southeast and raising a heavy swell. Reached Icy Cape about noon and found to our disappointment that, notwithstanding the openness of the season, further advance northeastward was barred by the ice. After the sky began to clear somewhat, and the rain to cease falling, we observed an ice-blink stretching all around the northern horizon for several hours before we sighted the ice, a peculiar brown and yellow band within a few degrees of the horizon. There was a dark belt beneath it, which indicated water beyond the ice.

We then turned westward, tracing the loose-drift edge of the pack until eight in the evening, when we turned to the east again, intending to await the further movements of the ice for a few days, and especially a change of wind to blow it offshore. There is a coal-vein between here and Cape Lisburne which we will visit and mine as much coal as possible, in case the weather permits. But as there is no shelter thereabouts, we may not be able to obtain any and in that case will be compelled to go to Plover Bay for our next supply.

About fifteen miles southwest of Icy Cape there is quite a large settlement [1] of Eskimos on the low, sandy, storm-swept shore. Cool and breezy must be their lives, and they can have but little inducement to look up, or time to spend in contemplation. Theirs is one

[1] Ututok?

constant struggle for food, interrupted by sleep and by a few common quarrels. In winter they hibernate in noisome underground dens. In summer they come out to take breath in small conical tents, made of white drill, when they can get it. They waved a piece of cloth on the end of a pole as we passed, inviting us to stop and trade with them. From Cape Lisburne up the coast to Point Barrow there is usually a two-knot current, but the wind and the ice have completely stopped the flow at present. The sun is above the horizon at midnight.

JULY 22   A dull, leaden day; dark fog and rain until about four in the afternoon; rained but a small fraction of an inch. About noon we once more sighted the ice-pack. The heavy swell of the sea is rapidly subsiding and the wind is veering to the northeast. We hope it will move the ice offshore and allow us to round Point Barrow. The pack is close and impenetrable, though made up of far smaller blocks than usual, owing, no doubt, to the mildness of last winter, and to the chafing and pounding of a succession of gales that have been driving over it at intervals all the spring. We pushed into it through the loose outer fringe, but soon turned back when we found that it stretched all around from the shore. By retreating we avoided the danger of getting fixed in it and carried away. Nearly all the vessels that have been lost in the Arctic have been caught hereabouts.

The approach to the ice was signalized by the appearance of walruses, seals, and ducks. The walrus is very abundant here, and when whales are scarce the whalers hunt and kill great numbers of them for their ivory and oil. They are found on cakes of ice in hundreds, and if a party of riflemen can get near, by creeping up behind some hummock, and kill the one on guard, the rest seem to be heedless of noise after the first shot, and wait until nearly all are killed. But if the first be only wounded, and plunges into the water, the whole "pod" is likely to follow. Came to anchor at half-past ten this evening, a little to the south of Icy Cape.

July 23   Clear and calm. Weighed anchor at eight in the morning and ran close inshore, anchored, and landed with instruments to make exact measurements for latitude and longitude, and to observe the dip. I also went ashore to see the vegetation, and Nelson to seek birds and look for Eskimo specimens. Found only four plants in bloom—saxifrage, willow, artemisia, and draba. This is the bleakest and barest spot of all. Well named Icy Cape. A low bar of sand and shingle shoved up by the ice that is crowded against the shore every year. Inside this bar, which is only a hundred yards wide, there is a stretch of water several miles wide; then, low gravelly coast. Sedges and grasses, dwarfed and frost-bitten, constitute the bulk of the flora.

We noticed traces of Eskimo encampments. There was blubber in abundance from a dead whale that had been cast up on the shore. They had plenty of food when they left. But before this they must have been hungry, for we found remains of dogs that they had been eating; also, white foxes' bones, picked clean. Found a dead walrus on the beach beyond the wreck of the whale.

At one in the afternoon we weighed anchor and turned north, crossing inside of Blossom Shoals, which are successive ridges pushed up by the ice, and extending ten or twelve miles offshore. In a few hours we reached the limit of open water. The ice extended out from the shore, leaving no way. Turned again to the south. Sighted the bark Northern Light[1] and made up to her. She showed grandly with her white canvas on the dark water, now nearly calm.

[1]A whaler.

The Cruise of the Corwin

Ice just ahead as we accompanied her northward while the Captain visited her. The sun is low in the northwest at nine o'clock. A lovely evening, bracing, cool, with a light breeze blowing over the polar pack. The ice is marvelously distorted and miraged; thousands of blocks seem suspended in the air; some even poised on slender black poles and pinnacles; a bridge of ice with innumerable piers, the ice and water wavering with quick, glancing motion. At midnight the sun is still above the horizon about two diameters; purple to west and east, gradually fading to dark slate color in the south with a few banks of cloud. A bar of gold in the path of the sun lay on the water and across the pack, the large blocks in the line [of vision] burning like huge coals of fire.

A little schooner[1] has a boat out in the edge of the pack killing walruses, while she is lying a little to east of the sun. A puff of smoke now and then, a dull report, and a huge animal rears and falls—another, and another, as they lie on the ice without showing any alarm, waiting to be killed, like cattle lying in a barnyard! Nearer, we hear the roar, lion-like, mixed with hoarse grunts, from hundreds like black bundles on the white ice. A small red flag is planted near the pile of slain. Then the three men pull off to their schooner, as it is now midnight and time for the other watch to go to work.

These magnificent animals are killed oftentimes for their tusks alone, like buffaloes for their tongues, ostriches for their feathers, or for mere sport and exercise. In nothing does man, with his grand notions of heaven and charity, show forth his innate, low-bred, wild animalism more clearly than in his treatment of his brother beasts. From the shepherd with his lambs to the red-

[1]The R. B. Handy, Captain Winants.

handed hunter, it is the same; no recognition of rights—only mur-
der in one form or another.

JULY 24   A lovely morning, sunful, calm, clear; a broad
swath of silver spangles in the path of the sun; ice-blink to the
north; a pale sky to the east and around to the south and west; blue
above, not deep blue; several ships in sight. Sabbath bells are all
that is required to make a Sabbath of the day.

Ran inshore opposite the Eskimo village; about a hundred
came off. Good-natured as usual. A few biscuits and a little coaxing
from the sailors made them sing and dance. The Eskimo women
laughed as heartily at the curious and extravagant gestures of the
men as any of the sailors did. They were anxious to know what was
the real object of the Corwin's cruise, and when the steam whaler
Belvedere hove in sight they inquired whether she had big guns
and was the same kind of ship. Our interpreter explained as well as
he could.

In the afternoon we had the Sea Breeze, the Sappho, the
Northern Light, and the schooner about us. The steam whaler had
only six whales. He had struck ten, taken four, and found two dead.
Last year he took twenty-seven. The whales were in windrows then;
at one time twenty-five were so near that no gaps between them
were so wide but that a man could strike on either side. They were
more abundant last year on the American coast; this year, on the
Asiatic. They are always more abundant in spring and fall than
during the summer.

Had a graphic account, from Captain Owen, of the loss of the
thirty-three ships of the whaling fleet near Point Barrow in 1874.
Caution inculcated by such experiences. Anchored this evening
near the Belvedere and four other vessels. The schooner people
complain that this is a bad year for "walrusing"; ice too thin; after

killing a few the hot blood so weakens the ice that in their struggles they break it and then fall in and sink.

JULY 25   Steamed northward again, intending, after reaching the ice, to make an effort to go to Point Barrow with the steam launch, and the lifeboat in tow, to seek the Daniel Webster, and offer aid if necessary. [This whaler is] now shut in about Point Belcher. We found, however, that the ice was shoved close inshore south of Icy Cape, and extended in a dense pack from there to the southwest, leaving no boat channel even. This plan was therefore abandoned with great reluctance, and we again moved southward, intending to coal, if the weather allowed, near Cape Lisburne. Calm, lovely night; slight breeze; going slowly under sail alone.

JULY 26   Lovely day; gentle breeze. Eight vessels in sight this morning. The Belvedere got under sail and is proceeding southward with us. Mirages in wonderful variety; ships pulled up and to either side, out of all recognition; the coast, with snowpatches as gaps, pulled up and stratified; the snow looking like arched openings in a dark bridge above the waters. About nine-thirty we noticed a rare effect just beneath the sun—a faint, black, indefinite, cloud-like bar extended along the horizon, and immediately beyond this dark bar there was a strip of bright, keenly defined colors like a showy spectrum, containing nearly all the colors of the rainbow.

JULY 27   A lovely day, bright and calm and warm. Coaling ship from a vein in a sandstone cliff twenty miles northeast of Cape Lisburne. In company with the Belvedere. Seeking fossils. Discovered only two species of plants. Coal abundant. Mined, took out, and brought on board fifteen tons to-day. The Belvedere also is coaling and taking on water. Three Eskimo canoes came from the south this evening and camped at the stream which flows into the sea on the north side of the coal bluff. The dogs followed the canoes alongshore. After camping they came alongside, but not before their repeated signs of peace, consisting of throwing up hands and shouting "Tima," were answered by the officer of the deck. This custom seems to be dying out, also that of embracing and nose-rubbing.

JULY 28   Lovely, tranquil day, all sunshine. Taking coal until half-past four in the afternoon. Then sailed toward Herald Island. I spent the forenoon along the face of the shore cliffs, seeking fossils. Discovered only four, all plants. Went three miles westward. Heavy snowbank, leaning back in the shadow most of the distance, almost changing to ice; very deep and of several years' formation—not less than forty feet in many places. The cliffs or bluffs are from two hundred to nearly four hundred feet high, composed of sandstone, coal, and conglomerate, the latter predominating. Great thickness of sediments; a mile or more visible on upturned edges, which give a furrowed surface by unequal weathering. Some good bituminous coal; burns well. Veins forty feet thick, more or less interrupted by clayey or sandy strata. Fossils not abundant.

While I was scratching the rocks for some light on the history of their formation, eight canoe loads of Eskimos with all their goods, tents, children, etc., passed close along the shore, going toward Icy Cape; all except one were drawn by dogs—from three to five to each canoe—attached by a long string of walrus hide, and driven by a woman, or half-grown girl, or boy. "Ooch, ooch, ooch," they said, while urging them along. They dragged the canoe with perhaps two tons altogether at two and one half miles per hour. When they came to a sheer bluff the dogs swam and the drivers got into the canoe until the beach again admitted of tracking. The canoe that had no dogs was paddled and rowed by both men and women. One woman, pulling an oar on the starboard bow, was naked to the waist. They came from Point Hope, and arrived last evening at a camping-ground on the edge of a stream opposite the Corwin's anchorage. This morning they had eight tents and all the food, canoes, arms, dogs, babies, and rubbish that belong to a village. The encampment looked like a settled village that had grown up by enchantment. Only one was left after ten in the morning, the occupants busying themselves caching blubber of walrus. In the sunshine some of the children enjoyed the luxury of running about naked.

Eleven-thirty; a calm evening. The sun has just set, its disk curiously distorted by refraction and light diminished by vaporous haze, so that it could be looked at, a glorious orb of crimson and gold with a crisp surface. . . . Horizontal layers of color, piled on each other evenly, made the whole look like cheeses of different sizes laid neatly one on top of the other. Sketched the various phases. It set as a flat crimson cake of dull red. No cloud; only haze, dark at the horizon, purple higher, and then yellow.

JULY 29   Calm, lovely, sunny day. Thermometer standing at 50° F. in the shade; warm in the sun; the water smooth with streaks; ruffled, like an alpine lake; mostly glassy, stirred with irregular breaths of air. Ice visible about noon, near "Post-Office Point."[1] Fine-grained, hazy, luminous mist about the horizon. A few gulls and ducks. Sun barely dipped beneath the horizon. Curiously modeled by refraction; bars dividing in sections always horizontal. Ducks flying at midnight.

JULY 30   Another glassy, calm day, all sunshine from mid-

---

[1] Said to be a point north of Bering Strait in the Arctic Ocean where, for some reason, the drift of oceanic currents is not strong. Whalers and other vessels customarily went there to exchange mail and news.

night to midnight. Kotzebue's gull, the kittiwake, about the ship; no seals or walrus. Herald Island came in sight about one o'clock. At a distance of eight to ten miles we reached the ice, but made our way through it, as it was mostly light and had openings here and there. But we suffered some hard bumps; pushed slowly and got close alongside, much to the satisfaction of the crew.

13

First Ascent of Herald Island

STEAMER CORWIN, OFF HERALD ISLAND, ARCTIC OCEAN, JULY 31, 1881   We left Herald Island this morning at three o'clock, after landing upon it and exploring it pretty thoroughly from end to end. On the morning of the twenty-fifth we were steaming along the coast a few miles to the south of Icy Cape, intending to make an effort to reach Point Barrow in order to give aid to the whaleship Daniel Webster, which we learned was beset in the ice thereabouts and was in great danger of being lost.

We found, however, that the pack extended solidly from Icy Cape to the southward and pressed so hard against the shore that we saw it would be impossible to proceed even with the steam launch. We therefore turned back with great reluctance and came to anchor near Cape Lisburne, where we mined and took on about thirty tons of coal. About half-past four in the afternoon, July twenty-eighth, we hoisted anchor and sailed toward Herald Island, intending to make a general survey of the edge of the great polar ice-pack about Wrangell Land, hardly hoping to be able to effect a landing so early in the season.

On the evening of the thirtieth we reached Herald Island, having been favored with delightful weather all the way, the ocean being calm and glassy as a mountain lake, the surface stirred gently here and there with irregular breaths of air that could hardly be called winds, and the whole of this day from midnight to midnight was all sunshine, contrasting marvelously with the dark, icy storm-days we had experienced so short a time ago.

Herald Island came in sight at one o'clock in the afternoon, and when we reached the edge of the pack it was still about ten miles distant. We made our way through it, however, without great difficulty, as the ice was mostly light and had openings of clear water here and there, though in some close-packed fields the Corwin was pretty roughly bumped, and had to steam her best to force a passage. At ten o'clock in the evening we came to anchor in the midst of huge cakes and blocks about sixty-five feet thick within two or three hundred yards of the shore.

After so many futile efforts had been made last year to reach this little ice-bound island, everybody seemed wildly eager to run ashore and climb to the summit of its sheer granite cliffs. At first a party of eight jumped from the bowsprit chains and ran across the narrow belt of margin ice and madly began to climb up an excessively steep gully, which came to an end in an inaccessible slope a few hundred feet above the water. Those ahead loosened and sent down a train of granite boulders, which shot over the heads of those below in a far more dangerous manner than any of the party seemed to appreciate. Fortunately, nobody was hurt, and all made out to get down in safety.[1]

[1]Captain Hooper's report of the incident and of Muir's skillful ascent of the island adds some interesting details:—

"Muir, who is an experienced mountaineer, came over the ice with an axe in his hand, and, reaching the island a few hundred feet farther north, opposite a bank of frozen snow and ice a hundred feet high, standing at an angle of 50°, he

The Cruise of the Corwin

While this remarkable piece of mountaineering and Arctic exploration was in progress, a light skin-covered boat was dragged over the ice and launched on a strip of water that stretched in front of an accessible ravine, the bed of an ancient glacier, which I felt assured would conduct by an easy grade to the summit of the island. The slope of this ravine for the first hundred feet or so was very steep, but inasmuch as it was full of firm, icy snow, it was easily ascended by cutting steps in the face of it with an axe that I had brought from the ship for the purpose. Beyond this there was not the slightest difficulty in our way, the glacier having graded a fine, broad road.

---

deliberately commenced cutting steps and ascending the ice cliff, the top of which he soon reached without apparent difficulty, and from there the top of the island was reached by a gradual ascent neither difficult nor dangerous.

"While approaching the island, by a careful examination with the glass, Muir's practiced eye had easily selected the most suitable place for making the ascent. The place selected by the others, or rather the place upon which they stumbled,—for the attempt to ascend was made on the first point reached,—was a small, steep ravine about two hundred feet deep. The jagged nature of its steep sides made climbing possible, and from the sea-level the top of this ravine appeared to these ambitious but inexperienced mountain-climbers to be the top of the island. After several narrow escapes from falling rocks they succeeded in gaining the top of the ravine, when they discovered that the ascent was hardly begun. Above them was a plain surface of nearly a thousand feet in height, and so steep that the loose, disintegrating rock with which it was covered gave way on the slightest touch and came thundering to the bottom. Some of the more ambitious were still anxious to keep on, notwithstanding the difficulty and danger, and I found it necessary to interpose my authority to prevent this useless risk of life and limb. A retreat was ordered, and with a good deal of difficulty accomplished. The descent had to be made one at a time, the upper ones remaining quiet until those below were out of danger. Fortunately, all succeeded in reaching the bottom in safety. In the meantime Muir and several others had reached the top of the island and were already searching for cairns or other signs of white men. Although the search was kept up until half-past two in the morning, nothing was found." (C. L. Hooper's *Report of the Cruise of the U.S. Revenue Steamer Thomas Corwin in the Arctic Ocean*, 1881, p. 52.)

First Ascent of Herald Island

Kellett, who discovered this island in 1849, and landed on it under unfavorable circumstances, described it as "an inaccessible rock." In general the sides are, indeed, extremely sheer and precipitous all around, though skilled mountaineers would find many gullies and slopes by which they might reach the summit. I first pushed on to the head of the glacier valley, and thence along the backbone of the island to the highest point, which I found to be about twelve hundred feet above the level of the sea. This point is about a mile and a half from the northwest end, and four and a half from the northeast end, thus making the island about six miles in length. It has been cut nearly in two by the glacial action it has undergone, the width at the lowest portion being about half a mile, and the average width about two miles.

The entire island is a mass of granite, with the exception of a patch of metamorphic slate near the center, and no doubt owes its existence, with so considerable a height, to the superior resistance this granite offered to the degrading action of the northern ice-sheet, traces of which are here plainly shown, as well as on the shores of Siberia and Alaska and down through Bering Strait southward beyond Vancouver Island. Traces of the subsequent partial glaciation to which it has been subjected are also manifested in glacial valleys of considerable depth as compared with the size of the island. I noticed four of these, besides many marginal glacial grooves around the sides. One side remnant [of a glacier] with feeble action still exists near the middle of the island. I also noted several scored and polished patches on the hardest and most enduring of the outswelling rock-bosses. This little island, standing as it does alone out in the Polar Sea, is a fine glacial monument.

The midnight hour I spent alone on the highest summit— one of the most impressive hours of my life. The deepest silence seemed to press down on all the vast, immeasurable, virgin land-scape. The sun near the horizon reddened the edges of belted cloud-bars near the base of the sky, and the jagged ice-boulders crowded together over the frozen ocean stretching indefinitely northward, while perhaps a hundred miles of that mysterious Wrangell Land was seen blue in the northwest—a wavering line of hill and dale over the white and blue ice-prairie! Pale gray mountains loomed beyond, well calculated to fix the eye of a mountaineer. But it was to the far north that I ever found myself turning, to where the ice met the sky. I would fain have watched here all the strange night, but was compelled to remember the charge given me by the Captain, to make haste and return to the ship as soon as I should find it possible, as there was ten miles of shifting, drifting ice between us and the open sea.

I therefore began the return journey about one o'clock this morning, after taking the compass bearings of the principal points within sight on Wrangell Land, and making a hasty collection of the flowering plants on my way. I found one species of poppy quite showy, and making considerable masses of color on the sloping uplands, three or four species of saxifrage, one silene, a draba, dwarf willow, stellaria, two golden compositæ, two sedges, one grass, and a veronica, together with a considerable number of mosses and lichens, some of them quite showy and so abundant as to furnish most of the color over the gray granite.

Innumerable gulls and murres breed on the steep cliffs, the latter most abundant. They kept up a constant din of domestic notes. Some of them are sitting on their eggs, others have young, and it seems astonishing that either eggs or the young can find a resting-place on cliffs so severely precipitous. The nurseries

First Ascent of Herald Island

formed a lively picture—the parents coming and going with food or to seek it, thousands in rows standing on narrow ledges like bottles on a grocer's shelves, the feeding of the little ones, the multitude of wings, etc.

Foxes were seen by Mr. Nelson[1] near the top of the northeast end of the island, and after we had all returned to the ship and were getting under way, the Captain discovered a polar bear swimming deliberately toward the ship between some floating blocks within a few yards of us. After he had approached within about a dozen yards the Captain shot at him, when he turned and made haste to get away, not diving, however, but swimming fast, and keeping his head turned to watch the ship, until at length he received a ball in the neck and stained the blue water with his blood. He was a noble-looking animal and of enormous strength, living bravely and warm amid eternal ice.

---

[1] In a recent article on "The Larger North American Mammals" Mr. E. W. Nelson has given the following account of this incident:—

"The summer of 1881, when we landed from the Corwin on Herald Island, northwest of Bering Straits, we found many white foxes living in burrows under large scattered rocks on the plateau summit. They had never seen men before and our presence excited their most intense interest and curiosity. One and sometimes two of them followed closely at my heels wherever I went, and when I stopped to make notes or look about, sat down and watched me with absurd gravity. Now and then one at a distance would mount a rock to get a better view of the stranger.

"On returning to the ship, I remembered that my notebook had been left on a large rock over a fox den, on the island, and at once went back for it. I had been gone only a short time, but no trace of the book could be found on or about the rock, and it was evident that the owner of the den had confiscated it. Several other foxes sat about viewing my search with interest and when I left followed me to the edge of the island. A nearly grown young one kept on the Corwin was extraordinarily intelligent, inquisitive, and mischievous, and afforded all of us much amusement and occasional exasperation." (*National Geographic Magazine*, November, 1916, p. 425.)

The Cruise of the Corwin

We looked carefully everywhere for traces of the crew of the Jeannette along the shore, as well as on the prominent headlands and cliffs about the summit, without discovering the faintest sign of their ever having touched the island.

We have been steaming along the edge of the pack all day after reaching open water, with Wrangell Land constantly in sight; but we find that the ice has been sheering us off farther and farther from it toward the west and south. The margin of the main pack has a jagged saw-tooth outline, the teeth being from two to ten miles or more in length, and their points reaching about forty miles from the shore of Wrangell Land. Our chances, however, of reaching this mysterious country some time this year seem good at present, as the ice is melting fast and is much lighter than usual, and its wind and current movements, after it breaks up, will be closely watched for an available opening.

14

Approaching a Mysterious Land

STEAMER CORWIN, OFF POINT BARROW, AUGUST 16, 1881 We left Herald Island at three o'clock in the morning of July 31. The clear water seen by me from the top of the island is called "the Hole" by whalers. I am told that it is remarkably constant in its appearance and position from year to year. What combination of currents, coast-lines, winds, etc., is the cause of it is not yet known. Neither is the Post-Office Point of ice understood.

On the day after leaving Herald Island the fine weather we had been enjoying for a week began to vanish, heavy cloud-piles grew about the horizon, and reeking fogs over the ice. We kept on around the serrated edge of the pack, and were glad to find a wide opening trending to the northwest, that is, toward the southmost point of Wrangell Land. Up we steamed, excited with bright hopes of effecting a landing and searching the shores for traces of the Jeannette. In the afternoon, while yet our way was tolerably clear, and after the land had been long in sight, we were enveloped in fog, and hove to, instead of attempting to grope a course through the drift ice and running the danger of getting the ship embayed. A few seals, gulls, and walruses were observed.

Next day, August 2, the fog lifted early in the morning, when we got under way and pushed hopefully onward once more, with the mountains and blue foothills of the long-lost land in full view, until noon, making our way easily through the drift ice, dodging to right and left past the large masses, some of which were a mile or more in length. Then the fog began to settle again over all the wild landscape; the barometer was falling, and the wind began to blow with indications of a stiff breeze that would probably press the ice toward the shore. Under these conditions we dared not venture farther, but loath to turn back we made fast to an ice-floe and waited developments. The fog partially cleared again, which induced us to make another short push ahead, but our hopes were again and again baffled by darkness and close-packed ice, and we were at length compelled to seek the open water once more, and await a general calm and clearance.

A piece of wood twenty-seven inches long, cut with a sharp axe, was picked up in the morning within, perhaps, twenty-five miles of Wrangell Land. It was evident, by its length and by the way it was split and cut, that it was intended for firewood. It seemed clearly to be the work of white men, possibly of some of the Jeannette's crew. But the grand excitement of the day, apart from the untrodden shore we were seeking, was caused by three polar bears, magnificent fellows, fat and hearty, rejoicing in their strength out here in the bosom of the icy wilderness.

When discovered they were regarding us attentively from a large cake of ice, each on a hummock commanding a good view of the ship, an object they no doubt saw for the first time in their lives. One of them was perched on top of a pile of blocks, the topmost of which was a pedestal square and level as if built up for an outlook. He sat erect and, as he was nearly the color of the ice, was not noticed until we were quite near. They watched, motion-less, for some time, throwing forward their long necks and black-tipped noses as if trying to catch and pass judgment on the scent of the big, smoking, black monster that was approaching them.

When we were within about fifty yards of them, they started, walked a step or two, and turned to gaze again as the strange object came nearer. Then they showed fear and began to lumber along over and across the wavelike rough hills and dales of the ice, afraid, perhaps, for the first time in their lives. For polar bears are the master existences of these frozen regions, the walruses being no match for them. First they broke into a lumbering trot; then, into a panicky, walloppy gallop, with fewer and fewer halts to look back, until they reached the far side of the ice-field and plunged into the water with a splash that sent the spray ten feet into the air. Then they swam, making all haste toward a larger floe. If they could have gained it they would have made good their retreat. But the steamer gave chase at the rate of seven knots an hour, headed them off, and all were shot without the least chance of escape, and without their being able to offer the slightest resistance.

The first one overtaken was killed instantly at the second shot, which passed through the brain. The other two were fired at by five fun-, fur-, and fame-seekers, with heavy breech-loading rifles, about forty times ere they were killed. From four to six bullets passed through their necks and shoulders before the last through the brain put an end to their agony. The brain is small and not easily penetrated, except from the side of the head, while their bodies may be shot through and through a score of times, apparently, without disabling them for fighting or swimming. When a bullet went through the neck, they would simply shake their heads without making any sort of outcry, the effect being simply to hasten their flight. The same was true of most other wounds. But occasionally, when struck in the spine, or shoulder, the pain would make them roar, and groan, and turn to examine the spot, or to snap at the wound as if seeking an enemy. They would dive occasionally, and swim under water a few yards. But, being out of breath, they were always compelled to come up in a minute or so. They had no chance whatever for their lives, and the whole affair was as safe and easy a butchery as shooting cows in a barnyard from the roof of the barn. It was prolonged, bloody agony, as clumsily and heartlessly inflicted as it could well be, except in the case of the first, which never knew what hurt him.

The Eskimos hunt and kill them for food, going out to meet them on the ice with spears and dogs. This is merely one savage living on another. But how civilized people, seeking for heavens and angels and millenniums, and the reign of universal peace and love, can enjoy this red, brutal amusement, is not so easily accounted for. Such soft, fuzzy, sentimental aspirations, and the frame of mind that can reap giggling, jolly pleasure from the blood and agony and death of these fine animals, with their humanlike groans, are too devilish for anything but hell. Of all the animals man is at once the worst and the best.

Two of the bears were hoisted on board, the other was neglected until it could not be found. Then came the vulgar business of skinning and throwing the mangled carcasses back into the clean blue water among the ice. The skins were stretched on frames to be dried and taken home to show angelic sweethearts the evidence of pluck and daring.

The Indians sometimes adorn their belts with the claws of bears and place their skulls about the graves of the men who killed them. I have seen as many as eighteen set about the skeleton of an Eskimo hunter, making for his bones an oval enclosure like a frame of shells set around a grave. The strength of the polar bear is in proportion to the massiveness of his limbs. The view of their limb muscles, swelling in braided bosses, could not fail to awaken admiration as they lay exposed on the deck. Such is the strength of the large bears, which are nine to ten feet long, that they can stand on the edge of an ice-floe and drag up out of the water a walrus weighing more than a thousand pounds.

The feet of the larger one measured nine and a half inches across behind the toes. They have long hair on the soles and around the sides of the feet for warmth in the dreary solitudes which they inhabit. When standing, the claws are not visible; the whole foot seems to be a large mop of hair spreading all around. The expression of the eye is rather mild and doglike in the shape of the muzzle and the droop of the lips, and only the teeth would suggest his character as a killer.

The third of August was spent in groping anxiously landward again through fog and ice until about six in the evening, when we reached the heavy, unbroken edge of the coast ice, at a distance of about twenty-five miles from the nearest point of land, and all hope of advancing farther was now at an end. We, therefore, turned away, determined to bide our time, hoping that warm winds and waves would at length melt and smash the heavy fields alongshore some time before the setting-in of winter. Nor were we altogether without hope of finding open water leading around the west shore of Wrangell Land. We soon found, however, that the pack stretched continuously across to Cape North on the Siberian coast, thus promptly forbidding all efforts in that direction.

The bottom of the ocean in that region is very level. Soundings made every hour for three days[1] varied scarcely more than five fathoms, and for half a day not one fathom. We saw several small fishes among the ice at our nearest point to lee; also seals, both saddleback and hair. Just as we were turning we discovered a bear

---

[1] In an average depth of twenty-one fathoms.

observing us from a large field of ice. He kept coming nearer a few steps and then halting to catch the smell of the ship. We did not attempt to kill him, however, as the advantage we had was not great enough. We could not chase him here with the steamer.

On the morning of the fourth we discovered a ship's foreyard with bits of rope still attached to it in such a way as to show that it had been carried away while the sail was bent. It seemed to have been ground in the ice for a winter or two, and probably belonged to one of the missing whalers.

After cruising along the Siberian coast for a few days, and calling at the Cape Wankarem village to procure as many as possible of the articles taken by the natives from the wreck of one of the lost whalers, we found ourselves once more on the edge of Wrangell ice, and again in dense fog on the morning of the ninth of August. A huge white bear came swimming through the drizzle and gloom and black heaving waves toward the ship as we lay at anchor, guided doubtless by scent. He was greeted by a volley of rifle balls, no one of which injured him, however, and fortunately he could not be pursued.

The fog lasted in dismal thickness until one o'clock on the morning of the eleventh, when we once more saw the hills and dales of Wrangell Land hopefully near. We discovered a lead that enabled us to approach within perhaps fifteen miles of the nearest portion of the coast. At times we thought ourselves much nearer, when the light, falling favorably, would bring out many of the smaller features, such as the subordinate ridges on the faces of the mountains and hills, the small dimpling hollows with their different shades of color, furrows that seemed the channels of small streams, and the peculiar rounded outlines due to glacial action. Then pushing eagerly through the huge drifting masses toward the nearest cape, judging by the distinctness of its features, it would suddenly seem to retreat again into the blue distance, and some other point catching the sunlight would be seen rising grandly across the jagged, hummocky ice-plain, relieved against the blue shadowy portions to right and left as a background.

It was not long, however, after tracing one lead after another, and coming always to a standstill with the ship's prow against ice of enormous thickness, before we were forced to the conclusion that all efforts made hereabouts would now be vain. The ice did not seem to have been broken or moved in any way for years. We turned, therefore, and made our way back to open water with difficulty and steamed along the edge of the pack to the northeastward. After a few hours' run we found the ice more promising, for it showed traces of having been well crushed and pounded, enabling us to bear gradually in toward the land through a wedge-shaped lead about twenty miles in length.

At half-past five in the afternoon we were again brought to a standstill against heavy ice, but this time within about five miles of the shore. We now felt pretty sure that we would be able to make a landing, and the questions that we wanted to put to this land of mystery came thronging to mind. This being, perhaps, the most likely place to find traces of the Jeannette expedition, in case any portion of this island was reached, would we find such traces? Has the country any human inhabitants? Would we find reindeer or musk oxen? What birds shall we find? What plants, rocks, streams, etc.?

We intended to walk the five miles of ice, dragging a light skin-covered boat with us to cross any open spot that we might come to; but ere we could set off, the fog began to settle gloomily down over the land and we determined to wait until the next morning, and in the meantime steam back out of the narrow, ice-jammed throat of the lead a few miles to a safer position, in case the ice should close upon us. Just as we turned from our nearest point of approach, we fired a cannon to stir the echoes among the hills and give notice of our presence in case anybody was near to listen.

The next morning, steaming ahead once more to the end of our water-lane, we were rejoiced to find that though there were now about eight or ten miles of ice separating us from the shore, it was less firmly packed, and our little vessel made a way through it without difficulty, until we were within two miles of the shore, when we found the craggy blocks extremely hard and wedged closely. But a patch of open water near the beach, now plainly in sight, tempted us to continue the struggle, and with the throttle wide open the barrier was forced. By ten o'clock in the morning the Corwin was riding an anchor less than a cable's length from a dry, gravel bar, stretching in front of the mouth of a river. The long battle we had fought with the ice was now fairly won, and neither the engine nor the hull of the ship seemed to have suffered any appreciable damage from the terrible shocks and strains they had undergone.

15

The Land of the White Bear

STEAMER CORWIN, WRANGELL LAND, AUGUST 12, 1881   A notable addition was made to the national domain when Captain Calvin L. Hooper landed on Wrangell Land,[1] and took formal possession of it in the name of the United States. We landed near the southeast cape, at the mouth of a river, in latitude 71° 4′, longitude 177° 40′ 30″ W. The extent of the new territory thus acquired is not definitely known, nor is likely to be for many a century, or until some considerable change has taken place in the polar climate, rendering the new land more attractive and more accessible. For at present even its southmost portion is almost constantly beset with ice of a kind that renders it all but inaccessible during both the winter and summer, while to the northward it extends far into the frozen ocean.

Going inland, along the left bank of the river, we found it much larger than it at first appeared to be. There was no snow left on the lowlands or any of the hills or mountains in sight, excepting the remnants of heavy drifts; nevertheless, it was still about seventy-five yards wide, twelve feet deep, and was flowing on with a clear, stately current, at a speed of about three miles an hour. While the

---

[1]The landing was made August 12, 1881.

snow is melting it must be at least two hundred yards wide and twenty feet deep, and its sources must lie well back in the interior of the island.

Not the slightest trace, however, could we find along the river, along the shore, or on the bluff to the northeastward, of the Jeannette party, or of any human inhabitant. A land more severely solitary could hardly be found anywhere on the face of the globe.

The beach was well tracked by polar bears, but none of the party could discover any sign of reindeer or musk oxen, though the country seems to abound in the kind of food they require. A single fox track was observed, and some burrows of a species of spermophile;[1] also a number of birds,[2] and about twenty species of plants,[3] most of them in bloom. The rock is clay slate, which weathers smoothly, and is covered with a sparse growth of mosses, lichens, and flowering plants, not unlike that of the adjacent coasts of Siberia and Alaska.

Some small fragments of knowledge concerning this mysterious country have been in existence for nearly a century, mostly,

[1] E. W. Nelson, in *Mammals of Northern Alaska* (1886), identified this spermophile as *Spermophilus empetra empetra* (Pallas), and remarks, "upon the hill where we planted our flag on Wrangell Island were many of their burrows."
[2] The following birds were observed by Mr. Nelson on Wrangell Land and Herald Island: Snow Bunting, Snowy Owl, Pacific Golden Plover, Pectoral Sandpiper, Red Phalarope, some kind of wild goose (perhaps Black Brant), King Eider Duck, Red-faced Cormorant, Ivory Gull, Pacific Kittiwake, Glaucous Gull, Glaucous-winged Gull, Ross's Gull, Sabine's Gull, Pomarine Jaeger, Long-tailed Jaeger, Rodgers's Fulmar, Horned Puffin, Crested Auk, Black Guillemot, Pigeon Guillemot, Thick-billed Guillemot, and a dead specimen of the Crested Shrike. This list is made from E. W. Nelson's *Birds of Bering Sea and the Arctic Ocean*, published with Muir's botanical observations in Treasury Department Document No. 429 (1883).
[3] See "Botanical Notes."

however, of so vague and foggy a character as to be scarce at all available as geography, while up to the time of Captain Hooper's visit no explorer so far as known had set foot on it. In the year 1820 Lieutenant Wrangell was ordered by Alexander, Emperor of Russia, to proceed from the mouth of the Kolyma as far as Cape Schelagskoj, and from thence in a northerly direction over the ice with sledges drawn by dogs, to ascertain whether an inhabited country existed in that quarter, as asserted by the Chukchis and others.

But the land in question was far from being generally known even by tradition among the Chukchis inhabiting the Siberian coast nearest to it. Wrangell seems to have found only one person during his long search for this land that had heard or could tell him anything concerning it. This man, an intelligent chief or head of a family, drew with charcoal a correct sketch of Cape Schelagskoj, Aratuan Island, and another to the east of the Cape, and then assured Wrangell in the most positive manner that there was no other island along the coast. When asked whether there was any other land to the north beyond the visible horizon, he seemed to reflect a little, and then said that, between Cape Schelagskoj and Cape North, there was a part of the coast where, from some cliffs near the mouth of a river, one might on a clear summer day descry snow-covered mountains at a great distance to the north, but that in winter it was impossible to see so far. He said also that formerly herds of reindeer sometimes came across the ice, probably from thence, but that they had been frightened back by hunters and wolves. He claimed to have himself once seen a herd returning to the north in this way in April, and followed them in a sledge drawn by two deer for a whole day until the roughness of the ice forced him to turn back. His opinion was that these distant mountains he had seen were not on an island, but on an extensive land similar to his own country.

He had been told by his father that a Chukchi elder had once gone there with a few followers in large boats, but what they found there, or whether they ever returned, he did not know. Still he maintained that the distant land was inhabited, and adduced as proof of it that some years ago a dead whale was found at Aratuan Island pierced by spears pointed with slate; and as his people did not use such weapons he supposed that the whale must have been killed by the people of the northland.

After spending three winters Baron Wrangell wrote concerning this country: "Our return to Nishne Kolymsk closed the series of attempts made by us to discover a northern land, which though not seen by us, may nevertheless exist, and be attainable under a combination of very favorable circumstances, the principal of which would be a long, cold, and stormless winter, and a late spring. If another attempt should be made, it would be advisable to leave the coast about Cape Yakán, which all the native accounts concur in representing as the nearest point to the supposed northern region."

STEAMER CORWIN, OFF POINT BARROW, ALASKA, AUGUST 17, 1881   The Corwin made a very short stay at Wrangell Land, partly because of the condition of the ice, which threatened to shut us in; and partly because it seemed improbable that a prolonged search in the region about our landing-point could in any way advance the main objects of the expedition. A considerable stretch of the bluff coast where we landed was scanned closely as we approached. Captain Hooper, Mr. Nelson, and myself examined a mile or two of the left bank of the river, a gently sloping hillside back from the river, and a stretch of smooth beach at its mouth. Meanwhile a party of officers, after erecting a cairn, depositing records in it, and setting the flag on the edge of the bluff fronting the ocean, went northeastward along the brow of the shore-bluff to a prominent headland a distance of three or four miles, searching carefully for traces of the Jeannette explorers, and of any native inhabitants that might chance to be in the country; then all were hurriedly recalled, and we forced our way back through ten miles of heavy drifting ice to open water.

On the shore we found the skeleton of a large bowhead whale, an oak barrel stave, a piece of a boat mast about seven feet long and four inches in diameter, a double kayak paddle with both blades broken, and a small quantity of driftwood. Every bit of flotsam was much scoured and abraded, showing that the articles had long been exposed to the action of waves and ice.

Back on the hills and along the river-bank the tracks of geese, marmots, foxes, and bears were seen, but no trace whatever of human beings, though the mouth of a river would above all others be the place to find them if the country were inhabited or had been visited by Europeans within a decade or two. Not a stick of the driftwood seemed to have been turned over or stirred in any way, though, from the steepness of the slate bluffs for miles along the coast, and the heavy snowbanks drifted over them, this low, open portion of the shore is about the only place in the neighborhood where driftwood could come to rest on a beach and be easily accessible to natives or others while traveling along the coast either on the ice or on land, and where they would also find a good camp-ground and water.

A few yards back from high-water mark there is a low pile of broken slate, with level ground about it, where any traveler passing this way would naturally choose to camp. But the surface of the slate is covered with gray, brown, and yellow rock-lichens of slow growth, showing that not one of these stones had been moved for many a year. Again, neither the low nor the high ground in this vicinity is at all mantled with spongy tundra mosses and lichens like most of the Arctic shores over which a man might walk without leaving a footprint. On the contrary, it is mostly bare, presenting a soft clay soil, derived from the disintegration of slates, the scanty dwarf vegetation—saxifrages, drabas, potentillas, carices, etc.—occurring in small tufts at intervals of a yard or so, with bare ground between them, smooth and mellow and plastic, with gentle drainage, admirably adapted for the reception and preservation of footprints. Had any person walked on this ground any time in summer when the snow was gone, and where the drainage slopes are not too steep, his track would remain legible to the dullest observer for years.

   We concluded, therefore, that this part of the country was not inhabited. Nor should the absence of inhabitants be wondered at, notwithstanding they might be derived from the Siberian coast at long intervals in accordance with the traditions bearing on the question among the Chukchis, or even from the coast of Alaska about Point Barrow or Cape Lisburne. For, though small parties of Eskimos or Chukchis might reach the land on floes detached from the pack while they chanced to be out hunting seals, or in boats driven by stormwinds or otherwise, such parties would probably seek to get back to their old homes again, or would die of famine. The seal and walrus, the two animals on which the natives of the Arctic shores chiefly depend for subsistence, are not to any great extent available, inasmuch as the ice seldom or never leaves the south Wrangell shores, and journeys twenty or thirty miles long would have to be made over rough ice to reach them.

Reindeer and musk oxen may exist in some other portions of the country, but if they occur in such numbers as would be required for the support of any considerable population the tracks of at least some few stragglers should have been seen hereabouts. Migratory water birds are no doubt abundant during the breeding and moulting season, producing sufficient food to last through a few of the summer months, and there are plenty of white bears, huge animals weighing from ten to twenty hundred pounds. Most of them, however, roam far out from land on the rugged edge of the ice-pack among the seals and walruses, and even under the most advantageous circumstances polar bears are poor cattle to depend on for a living. They certainly do not seem to have been fed upon lately to any marked extent, for we found them everywhere in abundance along the edge of the ice, and they appeared to be very fat and prosperous, and very much at home, as if the country had belonged to them always. They are the unrivaled master-existences of this ice-bound solitude, and Wrangell Land may well be called the Land of the White Bear.

Commander De Long, in a letter to his wife, written at sea, August 17, 1879, said that he proposed to proceed north by the way of the east coast of Wrangell Land, touching at Herald Island, where he would build a cairn and leave records; that if he reached Wrangell Land from there he would leave records on the east coast under a series of cairns twenty-five miles apart. In a previous letter, dated July 17, 1879, he said:—

> In the event of disaster to the ship, we shall retreat upon the Siberian settlements, or to those of the natives

around East Cape, and wait for a chance to get back to our depot at St. Michael. If a ship comes up merely for tidings of us, let her look for them on the east side of Wrangell Land and on Herald Island. If I find that we are being carried east against our efforts to get north, I shall try to push through into the Atlantic by way of the east coast of Greenland, if we are far enough north; and if we are far south, then by way of Melville Bay and Lancaster Sound.

While evidently pursuing this plan, he was seen by the whaler Sea Breeze on the second of September, 1879, about fifty miles south of Herald Island, entering a lead in heavy ice, which probably closed in upon his vessel and carried him past Herald Island. The search we made over Herald Island shows pretty clearly that he did not succeed in landing there, for if a cairn had been built on any conspicuous point we could not have failed to see it, as we traveled over it all in good bright weather. Nor would the failure of this part of his plan be unlikely when it is considered that he was fifty miles from the island so late in the season as September, and when heavy ice a hundred feet thick was already about him, and packed around the island. Neither does it seem at all probable from what we have seen this summer that he could have been successful in reaching Wrangell Land so late in the season under so many adverse circumstances of weather and ice. That he did not build a cairn or leave any trace of his presence within a few miles of our landing point does not prove by any means that he did not reach Wrangell Land at all, or that cairns with records may not exist elsewhere to the northward or westward. But the point where we landed being the easternmost point of the lower portion of Wrangell Land, it would seem from his plans as well as from known conditions of the ice to be of all others the likeliest place to find traces of the expedition.

In the case of the loss of his vessel and his reaching the land farther up the coast, he would be likely, in following his plan of retreat, to travel southward past this east point where the ice is more broken and extends a shorter distance offshore than elsewhere— conditions that seem applicable to the last two years at least, judging by what we have observed. Even should he not have built a cairn on so prominent and comparatively accessible a point, likely to be discovered by relief vessels, he could hardly have been able to pass without leaving some sign on the bank of the river, whether he made efforts to mark his presence or not. In case the explorers passed their first winter on Wrangell Land, they might either try to cross over the ice to Siberia toward spring from some point to the westward of our landing, or in case they reached the easternmost cape, near the south extreme of the land, about midsummer, they would probably find it the most favorable point of departure in making their way to the Siberian coast with sleds over the shore pack, and thence in boats. But as no trace of the explorers appears here, and no tidings have been obtained concerning them from the Chukchis, this, with all the evidence discovered thus far, goes to show that the Jeannette expedition either did not reach Wrangell Land at all, or did not make any extended stay upon it.

Notwithstanding the improbability of finding the expedition, the Corwin would gladly have been fast to a stranded berg, for a few days at least, during the fine August weather we were enjoying at the time, in order to send out exploring and search parties along the coast fifty or sixty miles in opposite directions, and back into the mountains, to learn something about the topography, geology, and natural history of the country, and to determine as surely as possible whether the missing explorers had touched this portion of the coast. But in so doing we should have risked being shut in, losing the vessel, and thus making still another party to be searched for. Besides, we might then be prevented from making other landings farther north in case the ice should leave the shores in that direction, and from extending relief to other vessels that might stand in need of it among the ice of this dangerous sea.

The floe outside of our anchorage was drifting along shore to the northeast with a powerful current at a speed of fifty miles a day, the majestic movement being made strikingly manifest by large bergs that were aground in water sixty feet deep, standing like islands, while the main mass of the pack went grating past them. With so much motion in the ice, the open lane and the strip of loose blocks and cakes through which we had forced our way in coming in was liable to close at any time, making escape impossible, at least until some chance change in the winds and currents might result in setting us free.

As it was, we escaped with difficulty after both engine and hull had been severely tested, the lane by which we entered having almost vanished, and the point where we reached open water was several miles to the northward of our ingoing track. Had our retreat been cut off, we would not, perhaps, have suffered greatly for a year or thereabouts, inasmuch as we had nine months' provisions aboard, which, with what game we might chance to kill in the nature of seals, bears, and walruses, could easily have been made to last considerably longer. We also had plenty of reindeer clothing and pologs, bought with a view to spending a winter in the Arctic, in case it should be necessary to do so. Everything could have been landed under favorable auspices, and preparations could have been made in the way of building shelters and storehouses. Then we would have had a fine long opportunity to explore this grand wilderness in its untouched freshness during the remaining months of summer and all the winter, while the vessel might possibly have escaped being smashed if laid up at the mouth of the river, and by a hairbreadth chance have been gotten out next summer.

Perhaps the ice does not leave the shore free more than once in ten years. The small quantity of driftwood on the beach would seem to indicate open water at times, but it might have been brought in by shifting, tumbling ice, after being held fast and gradually worked inshore after years of change in its position among the shifting floes, without the occurrence of any perfectly free channel of communication with the open part of the ocean. Our plan of retreat would have been similar to that proposed by Commander DeLong, that is, to the coast of Siberia. The loss of the vessel, however, and any work and hardship that might follow would not have been allowed to weigh against any reasonable hope of finding the lost explorers and carrying relief to them. But it was decided that more could be done, in all probability, towards carrying out the objects of the expedition by keeping the Corwin free. Only about half of the workdays of the summer were spent as yet, the weather was mild, the ice melting, and we had good hopes of finding open water reaching well inshore farther north, through which some other portion of the coast might be found accessible where the danger of being permanently beset would be less, and from whence extended land journeys might be made. Our efforts, however, to get northward along the eastern shore of Wrangell Land have, thus far, been unavailing.

16

Tragedies of the
Whaling Fleet

STEAMER CORWIN, OFF POINT BARROW, AUGUST 18, 1881
Finding it impossible to get northward through the ice anywhere
near the east side of Wrangell Land, it was decided that we should
cross to the American coast to make another effort to reach Point
Barrow in order to learn the fate of the whale-ship Daniel Webster,
which, as I have stated in a former letter, was beset in the ice there,
and to offer assistance in case it should be required.

On the fifteenth, near Icy Cape, we spoke with one of the
whalers from whom we learned that the Daniel Webster was
crushed and sunk, that about half the crew had made their way
down the coast to near Icy Cape, where they found the Coral and
were taken on board, and that the others were still at Point Barrow
or scattered along the shore, unless picked up by some of the fleet
that were going north in search of them as fast as the state of the ice
would allow.

Captain Owen of the bark Belvedere had sent a letter to them
by one of the natives, directing them to build large driftwood fires
on the beach to indicate their positions, and assuring them that
relief was near. We had hoped that, though beset in the heavy,
drifting pack and carried northward helpless and rigid as a fly in
amber, some change in the wind and current might set them free.
But in discussing the question with an experienced whaler who had

lost the first ship that he was master of at the same place and in the same way, he said that he had given her up for lost as soon as she was known to be embayed.

On receiving this news we started for Point Barrow and found the way clear, the pack having been blown offshore a few miles, and a heavy current was sweeping to the northward. Tuesday, the sixteenth, was calm and foggy at times; large masses of beautiful ice, blue and green and white, of every conceivable form, like the bergs derived from glaciers, were drifting with the riverlike current or lying aground—the remnants of the grand pack that so lately held possession of all the sea hereabouts.

When we were passing Point Belcher and Sunarnara[1] we learned from the natives that the ice was offshore as far as Point Barrow and beyond, that several whale-ships were already there, and that all the men from the broken ship had been taken on board. For some time the fog was so dense and the huge bergs so abundant we were compelled to lie to and drift with the current; but shortly after noon the sun came out, making a dazzling show among the ice and silvery water. Then the conical huts of the Eskimo village on Point Barrow came in sight, and rounding the Point we found ourselves in the midst of quite a fleet of whalers, from whom we received the good news that, as we had been told by the natives, all the missing members of the wrecked crew had at length been picked up and were now distributed among the different vessels. A few of them have been permanently added to the crews of the rescuing ships lying here, and nine have been received on board of the Corwin.

The strip of water sometimes found between Icy Cape and

[1]Sinaru?

Point Barrow is perhaps the most dangerous whaling ground yet discovered. The ice is of tremendous thickness, a hundred feet or more, and its movements are extremely variable from season to season, and almost from day to day. It seldom leaves this part of the coast very far, some years not at all, and it is always liable to be driven close inshore by a few hours or days of strong wind blowing from any point of the compass around from north to southwest. When, as frequently happens, there is a margin of fixed ice along the shore the position of ships is most dangerous, for when the pack comes in and catches vessels in this ice-bound lane while trying to beat southward against wind and current, it closes upon them and crushes them as between huge crunching jaws. Should there be no fixed ice, then vessels may simply be shoved ashore.

It is not long since the first whale-ship passed Bering Strait, and yet no less than forty-seven have been crushed hereabouts, or pushed ashore, or embayed and swept away northward to nobody knows where, while many others have had narrow escapes.

Thirty-three were caught and lost in this way here at one time, thirteen the following season, and one last July, while two others barely made their escape the same day just as the fatal ice-jaws closed behind them. This last victim, the Daniel Webster, left New Bedford in November, 1880, passed through Bering Strait on the tenth of June, and was caught in the pack July 3. It seems from the account furnished us by the first mate that she was following up a lead of open water about five miles wide, between the main ocean pack and a strip of shore-ice, fancying that two other ships that she had been following the day previous were still ahead, and on whose movements the Captain, who had no experience here, this being his first voyage, was to some extent depending. These two leaders,

however, had turned and fled during the night without being observed, while the Daniel Webster kept on northward, until within
sight of the end of the water-lane, when she turned and attempted
to beat her way back. But wind and current were against her, the
huge ice-walls came steadily nearer, and at length closed on the
doomed vessel, carrying her away as if she were a mere bit of drift
timber. About an hour later she was crushed, and sank to her upper
deck in about twenty minutes. Then she fell over on her beam-
ends against the ice and soon vanished in the icy wilderness.

The Point Barrow Eskimos, keenly familiar with the actions
of the winds and currents on the movements of the ice, watched
the struggling ship, and came aboard before the ice had yet closed
upon her, like wolves scenting their prey from afar. Many a wreck
had they enjoyed here, and now, sure of yet another, they ran about
the ship examining every movable article, and narrowly scanning
the rigging and sails with reference to carrying away as much as
possible of the best of everything, such as the sails, lead pipe for
bullets, hard bread, sugar, tobacco, etc., in case they should have
but a short time to work.

She filled so quickly after being crushed that the crew saved
but little more than the clothes they were wearing. Some hard
bread, beef, and other stores were hastily thrown over upon the ice,
and one boat was secured. As soon as she was given up, the Eskimos
climbed into the rigging, and dexterously cut away and secured all
the sails, which they value highly for making sails for their large
traveling canoes and for covers for their summer huts. Then they
secured as much lead as possible and anything they could lay hands
on, acting promptly and showing the completeness of the appren-
ticeship they had served.

The Cruise of the Corwin

The ship was then about five miles from the Eskimo village, and the natives were allowed to assist in carrying everything that had been saved. Under the circumstances, in getting over the five miles of ice with such riches, they, like white men, reasoned themselves into the belief that everything belonged to them, even the chronometers and sextants. Accordingly, at the village a general division was made in so masterly a manner that by the time the officers and crew reached the place their goods had vanished into a hundred-odd dens and holes; and when, hungry, they asked for some of their own biscuits, the natives complacently offered to sell them at the rate of so much tobacco apiece. Even the chronometers had been divided, it is said, after being taken apart, the wheels and bits of shining metal being regarded as fine jewelry for the young women and children to wear. A keg of rum, that the officers feared might fall into the Eskimos' hands and cause trouble by making them drunk, was thrown heavily over on the ice with the intention of smashing it, but it was not broken by the fall. One of the Eskimos picked up the prize, to him more precious than its weight in gold, and sped away over the slippery crags and hollows of the ice with admirable speed, vainly pursued by the first mate, and at the village it disappeared as far beyond recovery as if it had been poured into a hot sand bank. As wreckers, traders, and drinkers these sturdy Eskimos are making rapid progress, notwithstanding the fortunate disadvantages they labor under, as compared with their white brethren, dwelling in so severe a climate on the confines of the frozen sea.

The entire crew numbered twenty-eight men. All except the second mate and two of the sailors started down the coast afoot, after waiting some time for the ice to drift offshore far enough to allow some of the other ships to come to their relief, or at least far enough to leave a passage for their boat. At the river Cogrua[1] ten of the party turned back, weary and hungry and discouraged, to Cape Smyth, to pick up a living of oil and seal meat until relieved, rather than face the danger of fording the river and enduring yet greater hardships. The others pushed forward. Directed by one of the natives, they went up the bank of the river about twenty miles from its mouth, to where it is much narrower. Here they forded without danger, carrying their clothes on their heads to keep them dry.

Both parties seem to have suffered considerably from hunger as well as from cold and fatigue. The seal and oil meals, which the natives of the different villages they passed good-naturedly allowed them to share, but ill-supplied the place of their old-fashioned, rough, and regular rations. They speak of having been reduced to the strait of eating roots and leaves of the few dwarf plants found along their way. At Point Belcher they were so fortunate as to find a traveling party of natives, who, after their shaman had duly consulted the spirits, supposed to be influential and wise concerning the affairs of this rough region, and reported favorably, agreed to take the party in their canoe southward to seek the whaling fleet, the pack having by this time commenced to leave the shore. By this means the wanderers reached the bark Coral in four days, at a cost of two rifles and some tobacco.

The others were kindly received by the Cape Smyth people and entertained until the ice left the shore. One of the three left at

---

[1]Kugrua, a river tributary to the Arctic Ocean at the Seahorse Islands, a little east of Pt. Belcher. According to John Murdoch, Kug'ru is the Eskimo name of the Whistling Swan.

Point Barrow, it seems, wandered southward alone and lost himself with fright and hunger. He was without food for five days, save what he could pick up from the sparse sedgy vegetation, and was nearly dead when discovered by a relief party from one of the ships. The natives, he said, refused to allow him to enter their huts, because his eyes were wild and he would soon be crazy. Fortunately, all are now cared for.

Newly discovered whaling grounds, like gold mines, are soon overcrowded and worked out, the whales being either killed or driven away. But whales worth four or five thousand dollars apiece are so intensely attractive and interesting that the grand game has been hunted in the face of a thousand dangers over nearly all the seas and oceans on the face of the globe. According to Alexander Starbuck, in his history of the American whale fishery, there belonged, in the year 1846, to the various ports of the United States six hundred and seventy-eight ships and barks, thirty-five brigs, and twenty-two schooners that were hunting whales. In 1843 the first bowhead whales taken in the North Pacific were captured on the coast of Kamchatka, and in 1848 the first whale-ship passed Bering Strait. This was the bark Superior, Captain Royce. A full cargo was easily obtained, because of the abundance and tameness of the whales.

The news, like a gold discovery, spread rapidly, and within the next three years two hundred and fifty ships had obtained cargoes of oil and bone here. This is, therefore, a comparatively new hunting ground. Nevertheless it is being rapidly exhausted. The precious bowheads are no longer seen in "long winrows," as described by an old whaleman familiar with the region. This year only twenty vessels are engaged in the business.

Tragedies of the Whaling Fleet

In 1871 thirty-three vessels were caught in one flock off Point Belcher and crushed or shoved ashore. One of them is said to have been "crushed to atoms," the officers and crew escaping over the ice, saving scarcely anything but their lives. In a few days after the sixth of August most of the fleet was north of Blossom Shoals, and worked to the northeast as far as Wainwright Inlet. Here the ships either anchored or made fast to the ice, which was very heavy and densely packed. On the eleventh of August a sudden change of wind drove the ice inshore, catching a large number of boats that were out in pursuit of whales, and forcing the ships to work inshore in the lee of the ground ice.

On the thirteenth of August the incoming pack grounded, leaving only a narrow strip of water, in which the fleet was imprisoned more and more narrowly until the twenty-fifth, when a strong northeast gale drove the ice a few miles offshore, and whale-catching went on briskly without fear of another imprisonment. But on the twenty-ninth a southwest wind again drove the ice inshore, and once more shut in the doomed fleet. The thirty-three vessels were scattered along the coast for twenty miles, more and more rigidly beset until the fourteenth of September, when they were abandoned—that is, those not already crushed.

The following protest, throwing a vivid light upon the subject, was written on the twelfth of September, and signed by all the captains before abandoning their vessels:—

POINT BELCHER, ARCTIC OCEAN. SEPTEMBER 12, 1871
Know all men by these presents, that we, the under-signed, masters of whale-ships now lying at Point Belcher, after holding a meeting concerning our dread-

ful situation, have all come to the conclusion that our ships cannot be got out this year, and there being no harbors that we can get our vessels into, and not having provisions enough to feed our crews to exceed three months, and being in a barren country, where there is neither food nor fuel to be obtained, we feel ourselves under the painful necessity of abandoning our vessels, and trying to work our way south with our boats, and, if possible, get on board of ships that are south of the ice. We do not think it would be prudent to leave a single soul to look after our vessels, as the first westerly gale will crowd the ice ashore, and either crush the ships or drive them high upon the beach. Three of the fleet have already been crushed, and two are now lying hove out, which have been crushed by the ice and are leaking badly. We have now five wrecked crews distributed among us, we have barely room to swing at anchor between the ice-pack and the beach, and we are lying in three fathoms of water. Should we be cast on the beach it would be at least eleven months before we could look for assistance, and in all probability nine out of ten would die of starvation or scurvy before the opening of spring.

All the officers and crews—twelve hundred and nineteen souls—reached the seven relief vessels that lay waiting their arrival outside the ice, and were distributed among them, these seven being the remnant of the fleet that passed through Bering Strait in the spring. The next summer only five of the thirty-three were seen, one of them comparatively uninjured. All the rest had been smashed, sunk, burned, or carried away in the pack.

Five years later, in 1876, the fleet consisted of twenty ships and barks, and of this number thirteen were embayed in the pack, twenty or thirty miles off Point Barrow. After waiting and hoping for the coming of a liberating gale as long as they dared, the masters decided that it was necessary to abandon their vessels. Out of three hundred and fifty-three persons, fifty-three remained with the ships, hoping to get them free in the spring; but not one of the ships, or of those who stayed on them, was ever seen again. The three hundred who left their vessels, after enduring great hardships, succeeded in making good their escape to the rest of the fleet waiting outside the pack—all save three or four who perished by the way.

There are now twelve whale-ships about Point Barrow in sight from the Corwin, and all that would be necessary to shut them in is a gale from the southwest. Still the great love of action, and the great love of money, compel the risk here and elsewhere over and over again. The Corwin is now about to go southward to coal, at the mine twenty miles east of Cape Lisburne; or, in case the weather should be too rough to land at the mine, which is on a bare, exposed portion of the coast, to Plover Bay. Then we will return to the Arctic prepared to make other efforts to get on the south and east shores of Wrangell Land.

17

Meeting the
Point Barrow Expedition

STEAMER CORWIN, PLOVER BAY, SIBERIA, AUGUST 15, 1881
We left icy, gloomy Point Barrow on the afternoon of the eighteenth, with fine Arctic weather, which held out good hopes that we would be able to lie two days at the mine twenty miles east of Cape Lisburne, in order to take out and get on board a sufficient quantity of coal to last the Corwin the remainder of the season in the Arctic. But by the time we got down the coast near the mine the weather was rough, with a heavy sea sending stormy breakers against the exposed coal bluff, rendering it impossible to land and work. And as there is no shelter whatever for a vessel anywhere in the vicinity, and no likelihood from any indications that the weather would improve, it was decided that we should proceed at once to Plover Bay, our next nearest coaling point.

This Arctic mine, the nearest to the North Pole, as far as I know, of any yet discovered on the American continent, produces coal of excellent quality in great abundance and easily worked. There are five principal veins, from two to ten feet thick, fully exposed on the face of a bluff about two hundred feet high, excepting some of the lower sections that are covered with icy snowbanks. The latter are derived from drift that comes from the wind-swept hills, and does not melt till late in the summer, or not at all. The lower exposed portions of all the veins are beaten and worn by the sea waves. There can scarcely be any doubt, from what I have seen of the formation in which it occurs, that this is a true carboniferous coal, and superior to the great bulk of the tertiary and cretaceous coal found on this side the continent farther south. The Corwin coaled here twice last summer, and again this summer, July 27 and 28. So also did the steam whale-ship Belvedere. During calm weather the crew of the Corwin can dig out and put in sacks, and bring off in boats, about thirty tons per day.

On the twenty-first we passed through Bering Strait in a dense fog without sighting either of the Diomede Islands, which even in weather clear elsewhere are almost constantly enveloped in fog, causing no little anxiety to the navigator, inasmuch as they stand directly in the middle of the narrow part of the strait. A third islet called Fairway Rock, together with the uncertain flow of the currents hereabouts, renders the danger all the greater. The larger Diomede is about six miles long, the other half as large, and Fairway Rock still smaller. All three are simply residual masses of granite brought into relief by glacial action before the strait was in existence. These rocks rise above the general level because of their superior strength considered with reference to the resistance they offered to glacial degradation.

Approaching the islands in thick weather, the first intimation the navigator has of his being near them, and of the direction in which they bear, is either from the winds which gurgle and reverberate in passing over them, or from the birds—auks, murres, and gulls—which dwell on the rocks in myriads, and come and go several miles into the adjacent waters to feed. To persons acquainted with their habits it is not difficult to determine whether their flight is directed homewards or away from home. Thus the natives who dwell on these gloomy, dripping rocks and visit the shores of the adjacent continents in their frail skin-covered canoes are directed. But how the birds themselves find their way, flying in arrowlike courses to their nests, when every direction seems to us the same, is truly marvelous.

On cloudy nights it is dark now at midnight. The sun sets before eight o'clock, but because it sinks only a few degrees below the horizon, the twilight lasts nearly all night. In a week or two, however, we shall have seven or eight hours of real night, for, of course, the transition from constant day to day and night is very rapid in these high latitudes. This new order of things will be delightful. A few days ago we saw two stars in the twilight, which to us was an exceedingly interesting event after two months of starless day. The glories of the midnight sun in this mysterious polar world are truly enchanting, but not nearly so much so as the glories of the *midday* sun in lower latitudes, succeeded by the glories of the night, the deep sky of stars and the grateful change and repose they bring.

After passing through the Strait we had two gray, howling days, with head winds and rain, and thick fog, through which the Corwin beat her way, or was held lying to, heaving and rolling somewhere between St. Lawrence Island and Indian Point, as near as could be made out at the time by dead reckoning, and guessing the speed of the northerly current. Lying to in a gale, enveloped in old fogs,[1] and with little sea-room, and variable currents, is any-

---

[1]Fogs that have lasted a long time and prevented the taking of observations for the position of the ship.

thing but pleasant, to say nothing of the tedious discomforts caused by the movements of the vessel, the unceasing see-saw, creaking, pitching, and complaining. At such times only the gulls, those light-winged rovers of the sea, appear to be patient and comfortable as they gracefully drift and glide over the wild-tossing waves, or circle on easy wing about the ship, veering deftly from side to side, and wavering up and down through the gray, sleety gloom.

On the morning of the twenty-fourth, when the fog lifted, we found ourselves far north of our supposed position; the flow of the current to the northward during the two preceding days having been nearly eighty miles. We arrived here at five in the afternoon.

Entering the harbor, we discovered the schooner Golden Fleece lying at anchor, and shortly afterward a party from her came aboard the Corwin, which proved to be Lieutenant Ray[1] and his company of Signal Service officers on their way to establish a station at Point Barrow—ten persons in all.[2] Mr. Ray seems to be the right man for the place. He hopes to be able to get his buildings up and everything put in order before the coming on of winter, making a home in that stern wilderness for three years.

Point Barrow is a low, barren spit putting out into the icy ocean, and, before the discovery of Wrangell Land, the northernmost point of the territory of the United States. For many years it was believed to be the northern extremity of the American conti-

---

[1]P. H. Ray.
[2]This was the International Polar Expedition to Point Barrow, Alaska. The report of the valuable series of scientific observations and explorations made from 1881 to 1883 at the Point Barrow Station was published as House Executive Document, No. 44, of the Forty-eighth Congress. Among the members of the party were John Murdoch and Middleton Smith.

nent. But the extreme point of the peninsula of Boothia proves to be a few miles farther north than this. At first sight it would seem a gloomy time to look forward to—three years in so remote and so severely desolate and forbidding a region, generally regarded as the topmost frost-killed end of creation!

But, amid all the disadvantages of position, these men have much in their lot for which they might well be envied by people dwelling in softer climates. There is the freshness of their field of research in natural history, the immense number of summer birds that visit this region to molt and rear their young; the fine opportunities they will have to study the habits of the reindeer on the tundras, and the magnificent polar bear among the ice—the master animal of the north. Then there is the chance to study the little-known western Eskimos, who have a village[1] on the point, numbering about two hundred persons.[2]

Advantage, too, I am told, will be taken of the opportunity offered to explore the Colville and Inland Rivers, both of them large streams, the one flowing into the [Arctic] Ocean about one hundred and thirty miles to the east of Point Barrow, the other into Bering Sea through Hotham Inlet and Kotzebue Sound. They are almost entirely unexplored. Some of their upper branches must approach each other, as the Eskimos ascend the Colville and, making a portage, descend the Inland River to Hotham Inlet every year to trade, or at the portage meet natives from the other river and trade there. The exploration of these rivers is a very interesting

[1]Nuwuk.
[2]An admirable study of these Eskimos was, indeed, made by John Murdoch, a member of the party, and published in House Executive Document, No. 44 (1885), and in the Ninth Annual Report of the Bureau of Ethnology (1892).

piece of work, and Mr. Ray tells me that he intends to make an effort to accomplish it at the earliest opportunity. Furthermore, he is ambitious to achieve something in the way of new discoveries out in the Polar Ocean to the northward of his station.

From the fact that a current sets northward past Herald Island, and keeps a long lane reaching far beyond Herald Island open every summer, while the ice remains jammed only a few miles off Point Barrow and Cape Yakán, Siberia, and some years does not leave the shores at all, it would seem that there is a land lying to the east of Wrangell Land, making a strait up which the northerly current flows, while the unknown land prevents any great movement in the ice immediately to the north of the American continent, as Wrangell Land [stays] the ice opposite Cape Yakán and the coast in its vicinity. Again, migratory birds in large flocks have been seen flying north from Point Barrow in the spring, and returning in the fall. Besides, certain vague reports, which may have their foundation in fact, have been in circulation to the effect that land in this direction has been actually seen by a whaler, who was well offshore to the northeastward from Point Barrow, in an exceptionally open season.

With the experience that he will gain among the ice at Point Barrow, and the resources at command in the way of good assistants, skilled native travelers, with good dogs and sleds, etc., Mr. Ray may possibly be able to cross over the ice to this land, if land there be. In any case, whatever journeys may be made, over the ice or over the land, in summer or in winter, some new facts will surely be gained well worth the pains, for no portion of the world is so barren as not to yield a rich and precious harvest of divine truth.

The Cruise of the Corwin

Nor will these men be likely to suffer greatly. The winter cold, when skillfully met in soft hair and fur, is not hard to bear, while in summer it is so warm that the Eskimo children run about naked. The piling up of the ice on the shore in winter and spring must make a magnificent border for a home; and the auroral curtains and the deep starry nights, lasting for weeks, must be glorious.

The Corwin towed the Golden Fleece to sea this morning, and we hope to finish coaling, etc., in a day or two, and set out once more to the shores of Wrangell Land.

18

A Siberian Reindeer Herd

Steamer Corwin, Plover Bay, Siberia, August 26, 1881
This morning a party from the ship went to the head of the bay
under the guidance of a pair of Chukchis to see a herd of reindeer
that they told us was there. The distance, we found, is about eighteen miles from the lower harbor, where the Corwin is at anchor.
The day was fine and we enjoyed the sail very much, skimming
rapidly along in the steam launch over smooth water, past the huge
ice-sculptured headlands and mountains that formed the walls,
and the deep cañons and valleys between them that swept back to
clusters of glacial fountains. The naturalist made desperate efforts
now and then to obtain specimens of rare auks, petrels, ducks, etc.,
which were flying and swimming about us in great abundance,
making lively pictures of happy, exuberant life.

The rocks bounding the bay, though beautiful in their combinations and collocations of curves and peaks, inflowing and
touching delicately, and rising in bold, picturesque groups, are,
nevertheless, intensely desolate-looking for want of trees, shrubs,
or vegetation dense enough to give color in telling quantities visible
at a distance. Even the valleys opening back from the water here
and there are mostly bare as seen at the distance of a mile or two,
and have only faint tinges of green derived from dwarf willows,
sedges, and heathworts that creep low among the stones. Yet here,
or in the larger valleys adjacent, where the main tributary glaciers

came into the Plover Bay trunk, and in other valleys to the north-eastward, large herds of reindeer, wild as well as tame, find sustenance, together with a few wild sheep and bears.

On the terminal moraine of the ancient glacier that formed the first main tributary of the Plover Bay glacier, some four miles from the extreme head of the bay, we noticed two small skin-covered huts, which our guides informed us belonged to the reindeer people we were seeking, and that we should certainly find them at home, because their herd was only a little one and found plenty of weeds and moss to eat in the valleys behind their huts without going far away, as the people had to do who owned big herds. At two days' distance, they said, where the valleys are wide and green, with plenty to eat, there is a big herd belonging to one of their friends, so big that they cover all the ground thereabouts; but the herd we were to see was only a little one, and the owner was not a rich man.

As we approached the shore, a hundred yards or so from the huts, a young man came running to meet us, bounding over the moraine boulders, with easy strength as if his limbs had been trained on the mountains for many a year, until running had become a pleasant indulgence. He was presently joined by three others, who gazed and smiled curiously at the steam launch and at our party, wondering suspiciously, when the interpreter had told our object, why we should come so far and seem so eager to see their deer. Our guides, who, of course, understood their prejudices and superstitions, told them that we wanted a big, fat deer to eat, and that we would pay them well for it—tobacco, lead, powder, caps, shot, calico, knives, etc., told off in tempting order. But they said they had none to sell, and it required half an hour of cautious negotiation to get them over their suspicious alarms, and [to induce them to] consent to sell the carcass of one, provided we would leave the skin, which they said they wanted to keep for winter garments.

Then two young men, fine, strapping, elastic fellows, threw off their upper parkas, tied their handsomely embroidered moccasins firmly across the instep and around the ankle, poised their long Russian spears, which they said they always carried in case they should meet a bear or wolf, and away they sped after the herd up a long, wide glacier valley along the bank of a stream, bounding lightly from rock to rock in easy poise, and across soft bits of tundra and rough sedgy meadows with long, heaving, undulating strides. Their gait, as far as we could see, was steadily maintained and was admirably lithe and strong and graceful. Their small feet and ankles and round tapered shanks showed to fine advantage in their tight-fitting leggings and moccasins as they went speeding over the ground like trained racers glorying in their strength. We watched them through field-glasses until they were about three miles away, during which time they did not appear to slacken their pace a single moment. They were gone about three hours, so that the herd must have been at least six or seven miles from the huts.

In the meantime we ate luncheon and strolled about the neighborhood looking at the plants, at the views down the bay, and at the interior of the huts, etc. We chatted with the Chukchis about their herd, about the wild sheep on the mountains, the wild reindeer, bears, and wolves. We found that the family consisted of father, mother, a grown daughter, and the boys that were after the deer. The old folks were evidently contented and happy in their safe retreat among the hills, with a sure support from their precious herd. And they were proud of their red-cheeked girl and two strapping boys, as well they might be; for they seemed as healthy and rosy and robust a group of children as ever gladdened the heart of Chukchi parents. The boys appeared to be part owners of everything about the house, as well as of the deer, for in looking through the huts we saw a few curious odds and ends that we offered to purchase, but were told, in most cases, that they could not sell them until the boys came back.

Their huts are like all we have seen belonging to the Chukchis as far north and west as we have been—a balloon frame of long poles hewn on two sides so that they might be bent outward, the points coming together not in the middle, but a little to one side away from the direction of the prevailing wind, which gives them a curious hump-backed appearance. This frame is covered with skin of the walrus, if it can be had; if not, then with sealskin or deerskin. No great pains are taken to keep them rain-proof, so that in wet weather they are oftentimes damp or muddy. But there is not much rain in the Arctic regions, and the deerskin pologs, or drawing rooms inside, are kept perfectly dry and snug, whatever the state of the main outer tent may chance to be.

The two huts at this place are smaller and more leaky and dilapidated than is common. The covering is composed of different kinds of skin, perhaps a thousand pieces sewed together, some of them with the hair on, the whole appearing as one colossal patchwork, as if made up of small scraps. The head of the family seemed to be a little ashamed of them, for he explained with the air of a man making an apology, that *he* did not construct them; they formerly belonged to some one else, and that soon after he came to take possession one of them was torn open by a hungry

A *Siberian Reindeer Herd*

bear that went in and frightened his wife and daughter and stole some grease.

The Chukchis seem to be a good-natured, lively, chatty, brave, and polite people, fond of a joke, and, as far as I have seen, fair in their dealings as any people, savage or civilized. They are not savage by any means, however, but steady, industrious workers, looking well ahead, providing for the future, and consequently seldom in want, save when at long intervals disease or other calamities overtake their herds, or exceptionally severe seasons prevent their obtaining the ordinary supplies of seals, fish, whales, walruses, bears, etc., on which the sedentary Chukchis chiefly depend. The sedentary and reindeer Chukchis are the same people, and are said to differ in a marked degree, both in physical characteristics and in language, from the neighboring tribes, as they certainly do from the Eskimos. Many of them have light complexions, hooked or aquiline noses, tall, sinewy, well-knit frames, small feet and hands, and are not, especially the men, so thick-set, short-necked, or flat-faced as the Eskimos.

After we had watched impatiently for some time, the reindeer came in sight, about a hundred and fifty of them, driven gently without any of that noisy shouting and worrying that are heard in driving the domestic animals in civilized countries. We left the huts and went up the stream bank about three quarters of a mile to meet them, led by the owner and his wife and daughter, who carried a knife and tin cup and vessels to save the blood and the entrails—which stirred a train of grim associations that greatly marred the beauty of the picture.

I was afraid from what I knew of the habits of sheep, cattle, and horses that a sight of strangers would stampede the herd when we met. But of this, as it proved, there was not the slightest danger; for of all the familiar, tame animals man has gathered about him, the reindeer is the tamest. They can hardly be said to be *domesticated*, since they are not shut in around the huts, or put under shelter either winter or summer. On they came, while we gazed eagerly at the novel sight—a thicket of antlers, big and little, old and young, led by the strongest, holding their heads low most of the time, as if conscious of the fact that they were carrying very big, branching horns. A straggler fell behind now and then to cull a choice mouthful of willow or dainty, gray lichen, then made haste to join the herd again.

They waded across the creek and came straight toward us, up the sloping bank where we were waiting, nearer, nearer, until we could see their eyes, their smooth, round limbs, the velvet on their horns, until within five or six yards of us, the drivers saying scarce a word, and the owner in front looking at them as they came up without making any call or movement to attract them. After giving us the benefit of their magnificent eyes and sweet breath they began to feed off, back up the valley. Thereupon the boys, who had been loitering on the stream-side to catch a salmon trout or two, went round them and drove them back to us. Then the deer stopped feeding and began to chew the cud and to lie down, with eyes partly closed and dreamy-looking, as if profoundly comfortable, we strangers causing them not the slightest alarm though standing nearly within touching distance of them. Cows in a barnyard, milked and petted every day, are not so gentle. Yet these beautiful animals are allowed to feed at will, without herding to any great extent. They seem as smooth and clean and glossy as if they were wild. Taming does not seem to have injured them in any way. I saw no mark of man upon them.

A Siberian Reindeer Herd

They are not so large as I had been led to suppose, nor so rough and bony and angular. The largest would not much exceed three or four hundred pounds in weight. They are, at this time of year, smooth, trim, delicately molded animals, very fat, and apparently short-winded, for they were breathing hard when they came up, like oxen that had been working on a hot day. The horns of the largest males are about four feet long, rising with a backward curve, and then forward, and dividing into three or four points, and with a number of short palmated branches putting forward and downward from the base over the animal's forehead. Those of the female are very slender and elegant in curve, more so than any horns I have seen. This species of deer is said to be the only one in which the female has horns. The fawns, also, have horns already, six inches to a foot long, with a few blunt, knobby branches beginning to sprout. All are now in the velvet, some of which is beginning to peel off and hang in loose shreds about the heads of some of them, producing a very singular appearance, as if they had been fighting a rag-bag.

The so-called velvet is a close, soft, downy fur, black in color, and very fine and silky, about three eighths or half an inch long, with a few hairs nearly an inch in length rising stiffly here and there over the general plushy surface. All the branches of their horns are covered, giving an exceedingly rich and beautiful effect. The eyes are large, and in expression confiding and gentle. The head, contrary to my preconceived notions derived from engravings, is, on the whole, delicately formed, the muzzle long and straight, blunt and cowlike. The neck is thin, tapering but little, rather deep, and held, while standing at ease, sloping down a little, and the large males have long hair on the under side. The body is round, almost cylindrical—the belly not at all bloated or bent out like that of a cow. The legs are stout, but not clumsy, and taper finely into the muscles of the shoulders and hips. The feet are very broad and spreading, making a track about as large as a cow's. This enables the animal to walk over boggy tundras in summer and over snow in winter.

In color they vary almost as much in some specimens as do cattle and horses, showing white, brown, black, and gray at the same time. The prevailing color is nearly black in summer, brownish-white in winter. The colors of the tame animals are not so constant as those of the wild. The hair is, when full grown, very heavy, with fine wool at the bottom, thus making a warm covering sufficient to enable the animal to resist the keenest frosts of the Arctic winter without any shelter beyond the lee side of a rock or hill.

After walking through the midst of the herd, the boys selected a rather small specimen to be killed. One caught it by the hind leg, just as sheep are caught, and dragged it backward out of the herd; then the other boy took it by the horns and led it away a few yards from the herd, no notice being taken of its struggles by its companions, nor was any tendency to take fright observed, such as would, under the circumstances, have been shown by any of the common domestic animals. The mother alone looked after it eagerly, and further manifested her concern and affection by uttering a low, grunting sound, and by trying to follow it.

After it was slain they laid it on its side. One of the women brought forward a branch of willow about a foot long, with the green leaves on it, and put it under the animal's head. Then she threw four or five handfuls of the blood, from the knifewound back of the shoulder, out over the ground to the southward, making me get out of the way, as if this direction were the only proper one. Next she took a cupful of water and poured a little on its mouth and tail and on the wound. While this ceremony was being performed all the family looked serious, but as soon as it was over they began to laugh and chat as before. The herd, during the time of the killing and dressing, were tranquilly chewing their cud, not noticing even the smell of the blood, which makes cattle so frantic.

One of our party was anxious to procure a young one alive to take home with him, but they would not sell one alive at any price. When we inquired the reason they said that if they should part with one, all the rest of the herd would die, and the same thing would happen if they were to part with the head of one. This they excitedly declared was true, for they had seen it proved many times though white men did not understand it and always laughed about it. When we indicated a very large buck and inquired why they did not kill that big one, and let the little ones grow, they replied that that big fellow was strong, and knew how to pull a sled, and could run fast over the snow that would come by-and-by, and they needed him too much to kill him.

I have never before seen half so interesting a company of tame animals. In some parts of Siberia reindeer herds numbering many thousands may be seen together. In these frozen regions they supply every want of their owners as no other animal could possibly do—food, warm clothing, coverings for their tents, bedding, rapid transportation, and, to some extent, fuel. They are not nearly so numerous in the immediate vicinity of the bay as they once were, a fact attributed to the sale of several live specimens to whalers.

19

Turned Back by Storms and Ice

STEAMER CORWIN, ARCTIC OCEAN, BETWEEN HERALD SHOALS AND POINT HOPE, SEPTEMBER 3, 1881   On the morning of August 27, having taken on board a full supply of coal and water, and put the ship in as good condition as possible, we left Plover Bay and turned once more toward Wrangell Land.

In passing Marcus Bay, a short distance up the coast from Plover Bay, the Captain wished to make a landing to give some instructions to our Chukchi interpreter and dog-driver, who lives here, concerning the dogs and sleds that were left at Tapkan. The weather was too thick, however, to allow this, and the ship was put on her course for the western Diomede Island, where we arrived, against a stiff head wind and through thick fog, shortly after noon on the twenty-eighth. We lay at anchor for a few hours, while the wind from the Arctic came dashing and swirling over the island in squally gusts.

In the meantime, while waiting to see whether the wind would moderate before we proceeded through the strait, we went ashore and greatly enjoyed a stroll through the streets and houses of the curious village here. It is built on the bald, rugged side of the island, where the slope is almost cliff-like in steepness and rockiness. The winter houses are wood-lined burrows underground, entered by a tunnel, and warm and snug like the nest of a field-mouse beneath a sod, though terribly thick and rancid as to the air contained in them. The summer houses are square skin boxes above ground, and set on long stilt poles. Neither the one nor the other look in the least like houses or huts of any sort. But those made of skin are the queerest human nests conceivable. They are simply light, square frames made of drift poles gathered on the beach, and covered with walrus hide that has been carefully dressed and stretched tightly on the frame like the head of a drum. The skin is of a yellow color, and quite translucent, so that when in one feels as if one were inside a huge blown bladder, the light sifting in through the skin at the top and all around, yellow as a sunset. The entire establishment is window, one pane for the roof, which is also the ceiling, and one for each of the four sides, without cross sash-bars to mar the brave simplicity of it all.

Most of the inhabitants, of whom there are perhaps a hundred, had just returned from a long voyage in their canoes to Cape Prince of Wales, Kotzebue Sound, and other points on the American coast, for purposes of trade, bringing back ivory and furs to sell to the Chukchis of Siberia, who in turn will carry these articles by a roundabout way nearly a thousand miles to the Russian trading post, and return with goods to trade back to the Diomede merchants, through whose hands they will pass to the Cape Prince of Wales natives, and from these to several others up the Inland River, down the Colville, to Point Barrow and eastward as far as the mouth of the Mackenzie River.

The Diomede merchants are true middlemen, and their village a half-way house of commerce between northeastern Asia and America. The extent of the dealings of these people, usually regarded as savages, is truly surprising. And that they can keep warm and make a living on this bleak, fog-smothered, storm-beaten rock, and have time to beget, feed, and train children, and give them a good Eskimo education; that they teach them to shoot the bow, to make and throw the bird spears, to make and use those marvelous kayaks, to kill seals, bears, and walrus, to hunt the whale, capture the different kinds of fishes, manufacture different sorts of leather, dress skins and make them into clothing, besides teaching them to carry on trade, to make fire by rubbing two pieces of wood together, and to build the strange houses—that they can do all this, and still have time to be sociable, to dance, sing, gossip, and discuss ghosts, spirits, and all the nerve-racking marvels of the shaman world, shows how truly wild, and brave, and capable a people these island Eskimos are.

The wind having moderated, we got away from the box-and-burrow village and through the Strait before dark; then we steered for the south end of Wrangell Land, and after a speedy and un-eventful voyage came in sight of the highest of the coast mountains, on the thirtieth at noon. Thus far we had not seen the ice, and, inasmuch as nineteen summer days had passed over it since our last visit, we hoped that it might have been melted considerably and broken up by the winds, so as to admit of a way being forced through it at some point up to the land, or so near it that we might get ashore by crossing over the coast ice, dragging our light skin boat after us in case we should come to lanes of open water.

In this, however, we were disappointed; for when three and a half hours later we came up to the edge of the pack it was found to all appearances unchanged. It still extended about twenty miles offshore; it trended as far as we could see in the same direction as was observed before, and it seemed as heavy and unbroken as ever, offering no encouragement for efforts in this direction. We therefore sailed along the edge of the pack to the eastward to see what might be accomplished towards our first landing place. We gazed at the long stretch of wilderness which spread invitingly before us, and which we were so eager to explore—the rounded, glaciated bosses and foothills, the mountains, with their ice-sculptured features of hollows and ridges and long withdrawing valleys, which in former visits we had sketched, and scanned so attentively through field-glasses, and which now began to wear a familiar look. The sky was overcast, the land seemed almost black in the gloomy light, and a heavy swell began to be felt coming in from the northeast. Towards night, when we were not far from our old landing near the easternmost extremity of the land, the Corwin was hove to, waiting for the morning before attempting to seek a way in. But the next day, August 31, was stormy. The wind from the northeast blew hard inshore, therefore it was not considered safe to approach too near.

At eight o'clock we were in sight of the ice opposite the northeast cape, and it seemed to be farther off the land than at our first visit, and no opening appeared, though the weather was so dim and rough that nothing could be definitely determined. Generally, however, the ice was now drifting against the east side of Wrangell Land, and coming southward to so great an extent that our chances of effecting another landing began to be less promising.

When we were within twenty miles of Herald Island we hove to, waiting better weather before entering narrow lanes and bays in the pack when so heavy a sea was running. The sky was dismal all the afternoon—toward night, dull, lurid purple—and the wind was blowing a gale. The ice-breaker, made of heavy boiler iron, was broken by the pounding of the waves, and had to be cut away, which is unfortunate at this particular time.

September 1 was a howling storm-day, through which we lay to, swashing and rolling wildly among white waves, and drifting southeastward twenty or thirty miles a day. The next day there was no abatement in the force of the gale up to two o'clock in the afternoon. A heavy sea, streaked with foam, was running parallel to the direction of the wind, while the air was filled with snow, adding to the wintry aspect of the day. While we were still holding on, hoping the storm would subside from hour to hour, one of the rudder chains parted.

This made Captain Hooper decide that in view of the condition of the ship, and the ice, and the weather, the risk attending further efforts this year to search the shores of Wrangell Land should not be incurred, more especially since the position and drift of the ice held out but little promise of allowing another landing to be made, or of a sufficiently near approach to enable us to add appreciably to the knowledge already acquired. Accordingly, after the rudder was mended as securely as possible, the good Corwin, excused from further ice duty, was turned away from the war and headed for the American coast at Point Hope.

Had the ship been in good condition, the battle would probably have been waged a few more weeks along the edge of the ice barrier, watching the appearance of any vulnerable point of attack, whatever the result might have been. Now it seems we are homeward bound. We intend to stop at Kotzebue Sound, St. Michael, St. Paul, and Unalaska to make necessary repairs, take on coal, etc., and we may reach San Francisco by the middle of October.

Turned Back by Storms and Ice

We have not met the Rodgers. We learned from the natives at Plover Bay that she had called there and left seven days before our arrival. That was August 17. We suppose she went to St. Michael from there to coal and take on provisions, which would probably require a week. If so, we may have passed the Strait ahead of her. But in case she had already been at St. Michael, then, in following out her instructions, she could trace the Siberian coast for some distance, making inquiries among the Chukchis, where she may possibly be at present. Or, if this part of the work of the expedition had been completed before the coming on of the gale, she may be sheltering about Herald Island or some point on the coast of Wrangell Land.[1]

[1]Mr. Muir's supposition proved to be correct. The U.S.S. Rodgers, Lieutenant R. M. Berry commanding, reached Wrangell Land, August 25, and found shelter the next day in a snug little harbor on the southeastern coast of the island. There the Rodgers remained until September 13, while two search parties explored the shores of the island for traces of the Jeannette expedition.

20

Homeward Bound

On the home voyage, all the hard Arctic work done, the Corwin stopped a week at the head of Kotzebue Sound, near Chamisso Island, to seek a fresh supply of water and make some needful repairs and observations, during which time I had a capital opportunity to examine the curious and interesting ice formations of the shores of Eschscholtz Bay. I found ice in some form or other, exposed at intervals of from a mile to a few yards, on the tide-washed front of the shore bluffs on both sides of the bay, a distance of about fifty miles. But it is only the most conspicuous mass, forming a bluff, at Elephant Point, on the south side of the bay, that seems to have been observed hitherto, or attracted much attention.

This Elephant Point, so called from the fossil elephant tusks found here, is a bluff of solid ice, one hundred and forty feet high, covered on the top with a foot or two of ordinary tundra vegetation, and with tall grass on the terraces and shelving portions of the front, wherever the slope is sufficiently gentle for soil to find rest. It is a rigid fossil fragment of a glacier leaning back against the north side of a hill, mostly in shadow, and covered lightly with glacial detritus from the hill slope above it, over which the tundra vegetation has gradually been extended, and which eventually formed a thick felt-like protection against waste during the summer. Thus it has lasted until now, wasting only on the exposed face fronting the bay, which is being constantly undermined, the soil and vegetation on top

[176]

being precipitated over the raw, melting ice front and washed away by the tide. Were it not that its base is swept by tide currents, the accumulation of tundra moss and peat would finally re-bury the front and check further waste. As it is, the formation will not last much longer—probably not more than a thousand or fifteen hundred years. Its present age is perhaps more than this.

When one walks along the base of the formation—which is about a mile or so in length—making one's way over piles of rotten humus and through sloppy bog mud of the consistence of watery porridge, mixed with bones of elephants, buffaloes, musk oxen, etc., the ice so closely resembles the wasting snout of a glacier, with its jagged projecting ridges, ledges, and small, dripping, tinkling rills, that it is not easy to realize that it is not one in ordinary action.

Mingled with the true glacier ice we notice masses of dirty stratified ice, made up of clean layers alternating with layers of mud and sand, and mingled with bits of humus and sphagnum, and of leaves and stems of the various plants that grow on the tundra above. This dirty ice of peculiar stratification never blends into the glacier ice, but is simply frozen upon it, filling cavities or spreading over slopes here and there. It is formed by the freezing of films of clear and dirty water from the broken edge of the tundra, a process going on every spring and autumn, when frosts and thaws succeed each other night and morning, cloudy days and sunny days. This, of course, is of comparatively recent age, even the oldest of it.

A striking result of the shaking up and airing and draining of the tundra soil is seen on the face of the ice slopes and terraces. When the undermined tundra material rolls down upon those portions of the ice front where it can come to rest, it is well buffeted and shaken, and frequently lies upside down as if turned with a plow. Here it is well drained through resting on melting ice, and though not more than a foot or two in thickness, it produces a remarkably close and tall growth of grass, four to six feet high, and as lush and broad-leaved as may be found in any farmer's field. Cut for hay it would make about four or five tons per acre.

Only a few other plants that would be called weeds are found growing among the grass, mostly senecio and artemisia, both tall and exuberant, showing the effects of this curious system of cultivation on this strange soil. The vegetation on top of the bluff is the most beautiful that I have yet seen, not rank and cultivated looking, like that on the face slopes, but showing the finest and most delicate beauty of wildness, in forms, combinations, and colors of leaf, stalk, and fruit. There were red and yellow dwarf birch, arbutus, willow, and purple huckleberry, with lovely grays of sedges and lichens. The neutral tints of the lichens are intensely beautiful.

I found the shore-bluff towards the mouth of the Buckland River from forty to sixty feet high, with a regular slope of about thirty degrees. It was covered with willows and alders, some of them five or six feet high, and long grass; also patches of ice here and there, but no large masses. The soil is a fine blue clay at bottom, with water-worn quartz, pebbles and sand above it, like that of the opposite side of the estuary, and evidently brought down by the river floods when the ice of the glaciers that occupied this river basin and that of the Kuuk[1] was melting.

The ice that I found here and on the opposite side of the bay, especially where the tundra is low and flat, let us say forty or fifty

---

[1] A river tributary to Eschscholtz Bay from the east. It was called Kuuk on British Admiralty charts of the early eighties, but is now known as the Mungoark River.

feet above the sea, and covered with pools and strips of water, is not glacier ice, but ice derived from water freezing in pools and veins and hollows, overgrown with mosses, lichens, etc., and afterwards exposed as fossil ice on the shore face of the tundra where it is being wasted by the action of the sea. The tundra has been cracked in every direction, and in looking over its surface, slight depressions, or some difference in the vegetation, indicate the location and extent of the fissures. When these are traced forward to the edge of the shore-bluff, a cross-section of ice is seen from two to four or five feet wide. The larger sections are simply the exposed sides of those ice veins that chance to trend in a direction parallel to the face of the bluff. Besides these I found several other kinds of ice, differing in origin from the foregoing, but which can hardly be described in a mere letter, however interesting to the geologist.

At St. Michael we found a party of wrecked prospectors from Golofnin Bay, who were anxiously awaiting the arrival of the Corwin, as she would be the last vessel leaving for California this year. This proved to be the Oakland party mentioned in a previous letter. With genuine Yankee enterprise [these men] had pushed their way into the far wilderness beyond the Yukon to seek for silver. Specimens of bright, exciting ore, assaying a hundred and fifty dollars to the ton, had been exhibited in Oakland, brought from a mine said to be located near tide water at Golofnin Bay, Alaska, and so easily worked that large ships could be loaded with the precious ore about as readily as with common ballast. Thereupon a company, called the Alaska Mining Company, was organized, the schooner W. F. March chartered, and with the necessary supplies a party of ten sailed from San Francisco May 5, 1881, for Golofnin Bay, to explore this mine in particular, and the region in general, and then to return, this fall, with a cargo of ore.

The Cruise of the Corwin

They arrived in Golofnin Bay June 18, lost their vessel in a gale on the north side of the bay August 15, and arrived in twenty-one days at St. Michael in canoes and a boat that was saved from the wreck. They found the mine as rich as represented, but far less accessible. It is said to be about thirty miles from tide water. All feel confident that they have a valuable mine. Two or three of the party were away at the time of the disaster, prospecting for cinnabar on the Kuskoquim, and are left behind to pass the winter as best they may at some of the trading stations.

Our two weeks' stay at Unalaska has been pleasant and restful after the long cruise—about fourteen thousand miles altogether up to this point. The hill slopes and mountains look richly green and foodful, and the views about the harbor, at the close and beginning of storms, when clouds are wreathing the alpine summits, are very beautiful.

The huts of the Aleuts here are very picturesque at this time of the year. The grass grows tall over the sides and the roof, waving in the wind, and making a fine fringe about the windows and the door. When the church bell rings on Sunday and the good calico-covered people plod sedately forth to worship, and the cows on the hillside moo blandly, and the sun shines over the green slopes, then the scene is like a bit of New England or old Scotland. But later in the day, when the fiery kvass is drunk, and the accordians and concertinas and cheap music boxes are in full blast, then the noise and unseemly clang attending drunkenness is not at all like a Scotch sabbath.

Most of the Aleuts have an admixture of Russian blood. Many of them dance well. Three balls were given during our stay here, that is to say, American balls with native women. The Aleuts have their own dances in their small huts.

Homeward Bound

A few days ago I made an excursion to the top of a well-formed volcanic cone at the mouth of a picturesque glacial fiord, about eight miles from here. This mountain, about two thousand feet high, commands a magnificent view of the mountains of Unalaska, Akutan, and adjacent islands. Akutan[1] still emits black smoke and cinders at times, and thunders loud enough to be heard at Unalaska.

The noblest of them all was Makushin, about nine thousand feet high and laden with glaciers, a grand sight, far surpassing what I had been led to expect. There is a spot on its summit which is said to smoke, probably mostly steam and vapor from the infiltration of water into the heated cavities of the old volcano. The extreme summit of Makushin was wrapped in white clouds, and from beneath these the glaciers were seen descending impressively into the sunshine to within a thousand or fifteen hundred feet of sea-level. This fine mountain, glittering in its showy mail of snow and ice, together with a hundred other peaks dipping into the blue sky, and every one of them telling the work of ice or fire in their forms and sculpture—these, and the sparkling sea, and long inreaching fiords, are a noble picture to add to the thousand others which have enriched our lives this summer in the great Northland.

[1]The highest mountain of Akutan Island. The United States Coast and Geodetic Survey Chart No. 8860 gives its altitude as forty-one hundred feet.

Appendix

Appendix

The Glaciation of the Arctic and Sub-Arctic Regions
Visited During the Cruise

The monuments of the glaciation of the regions about Bering Sea and the northern shores of Siberia and Alaska are in general much broken and obscured on account of the intensity of the action of the agents of destruction in these low, moist regions, together with the perishable character of the rocks of which most of the monuments consist. Lofty headlands, once covered with clear glacial inscriptions, have been undermined and cast down in loose, draggled taluses, while others, in a dim, ruinous condition, with most of their surface records effaced, are rapidly giving way to the weather. The moraines, also, and the grooved, scratched, and polished surfaces are much blurred and wasted, while glaciated areas of great extent are not open to observation at all, being covered by the shallow waters of Bering Sea and the Arctic Ocean, and buried beneath sediments and coarse detritus which has been weathered from the higher grounds, or deposited by the ice itself when it was being melted and withdrawn towards the close of the main glacial period. But amid this general waste and obscurity a few legible fragments, favorably situated here and there,

Appendix

have escaped destruction—patches of polished and striated surfaces in a fair state of preservation, with moraines of local glaciers that have not been exposed to the heavier forms of water or avalanche action. And had these fading vestiges perished altogether, yet would not the observer be left without a sure guide, for there are other monuments of ice action in all glaciated regions that are almost indestructible, enduring for tens of thousands of years after those simpler traces that we have been considering have vanished. These are the material of moraines, though scattered, washed, crumbled, and reformed over and over again; and the sculpture and configuration of the landscape in general, cañons, valleys, mountains, ridges, *roches moutonnées* with forms and correlations specifically glacial. These, also, it is true, suffer incessant waste, being constantly written upon by other agents; yet, because the glacial characters are formed on so colossal a scale of magnitude, they continue to stand out free and clear through every after inscription whether of the torrent, the avalanche, or universal eroding atmosphere; opening grand and comprehensive views of the vanished ice, and the geographical and topographical changes effected by its action in the form of local and distinct glaciers. River-like, they flowed from the mountains to the sea, and, as a broad, undulating mantle, crawled over all the landscape through unnumbered centuries; crushed and ground and spread soil-beds; fashioned the features of mountain and plain; extended the domain of the sea; separated continents; dotted new coasts with islands, fringed them with deep in-reaching fiords, and impressed their peculiar style of sculpture on all the regions over which they passed.

A general exploration of the mountain ranges of the Pacific Coast shows that there are about sixty-five small residual glaciers on the Sierra Nevada of California, between latitude 36° 30′ and 39°, distributed singly or in small groups on the north sides of the highest peaks at an elevation of about eleven to twelve thousand feet above the level of the sea, representatives of the grand glaciers that once covered all the range. More than

Appendix

two thirds of these lie between latitude 37° and 38°, and form the highest sources of the San Joaquin, Tuolumne, Merced, and Owens Rivers.

Mount Shasta, near the northern boundary of California, has a few shrinking glacier remnants, the largest about three miles in length. We find that, to the north of California, groups of active glaciers still exist on all the highest mountains—Mounts Jefferson, Adams, Saint Helens, Hood, Rainier, Baker, and others. Of these Mount Rainier is the highest and iciest. Its summit is fairly capped with ice, and eight glaciers, from seven to fifteen miles long, radiate from it as a center and form the sources of the principal streams. The lowest descends to about thirty-five hundred feet above sea level, pouring a stream opaque with glacial mud into the head of Puget Sound.

On through British Columbia and southeastern Alaska the broad sustained mountain chain extending along the coast is generally glacier-bearing. The upper branches of nearly every one of the main cañons are occupied by glaciers, which gradually increase in size and descend lower until the lofty region between Mount Fairweather and Mount St. Elias is reached, where a considerable number discharge into the waters of the ocean.

This is the region of greatest glacial abundance on the continent. To the northward from here the glaciers gradually diminish in size and depth and melt at higher levels until the latitude of about 62° is reached, beyond which few, if any, glaciers remain in existence, the ground being comparatively low and the annual snowfall light.

Between latitude 56° and 60° there are probably more than five thousand glaciers, great and small, hundreds of the largest size, descending through the forests nearly to the level of the sea, though, as far as I know after a pretty thorough exploration of the region, not more than twenty-five discharge into the sea.

All the long, high-walled fiords into which these great glaciers of the first class flow are of course crowded with icebergs of every conceivable form, which are detached at intervals of a few minutes. But these are small as compared with those of Greenland, and only a few escape from the intricate labyrinth of channels, with which this portion of the coast is fringed, into the open sea. Nearly all of them are washed and drifted back and forth in the fiords by wind and tide until finally melted by sunshine and the copious warm rains of summer.

The southmost of the glaciers that reach the sea occupies a narrow fiord about twenty miles to the northwest of the mouth of the Stikine River, in latitude 56° 50′. It is called "Hutli"[1] by the natives, from the noise made by the icebergs in rising and falling from the inflowing glacier. About one degree farther north there are four of these complete glaciers at the heads of branches of Holkham Bay, at the head of Taku Inlet one, and at the head and around the sides of a bay[2] trending in a general northerly direction from Cross Sound, first explored by myself in 1879, there are no less than five of these complete glaciers reaching tide-water, the largest of which, the Muir, is of colossal size, having upwards of two hundred tributaries and a width of trunk below the confluence of the main tributaries of three to twenty-five miles. Between the west side of this icy bay and the ocean all the ground, high and low, with the exception of the summits of the mountain peaks, is covered by a mantle of ice from one to three thousand feet thick, which discharges to the eastward and westward through many distinct mouths.

This ice-sheet, together with the multitude of distinct glaciers that load the lofty mountains of the coast, evidently once formed part of one grand, continuous ice-sheet that flowed over all the region hereabouts,

[1]Now known as Le Conte Glacier; also the Bay into which it discharges. Both were so named in 1887 by Lieutenant-Commander Charles M. Thomas, U.S.N., presumably in honor of Joseph Le Conte, the well-known California geologist. "Hutli" is the Tlingit Indian name for the mythical bird which produces thunder by the flapping of its wings. The word, therefore, means "The Thunderer."
[2]Now known as Glacier Bay.

extending southward as far as the Straits of Juan de Fuca, for all the islands of the Alexander Archipelago, great and small, as well as the headlands and promontories of the mainland, are seen to have forms of greatest strength with reference to the action of a vast press of oversweeping ice, and their surfaces have a smooth, rounded, over-rubbed appearance, generally free from angles. The canals, channels, straits, passages, sounds, etc., between the islands—a marvelous labyrinth—manifest in their forms and trends and general characteristics the same subordination to the grinding action of a continuous ice-sheet, and they differ from the islands, as to their origin, only in being portions of the general pre-glacial margin of the continent, more deeply eroded, and, therefore, covered with the ocean waters, which flowed into them as the ice was melted out of them.

That the dominion of the sea is being extended over the land by the wearing away of its shores is well known. But in these northern regions the coast rocks have been so short a time exposed to wave-action that they are but little wasted as yet, the extension of the sea affected by its own action in post-glacial time in this region being probably less than the millionth part of that affected by glacial action during the last glacial period.

Traces of the ancient glaciers made during the period of greater extension abound on the California Sierra as far south as latitude 36°. Even the most evanescent of them, the polished surfaces, are still found, in a marvelously perfect state of preservation, on the upper half of the middle portion of the range. They occur in irregular patches, some of which are several acres in extent, and, though they have been subjected to the weather with all its storms for thousands of years, their mechanical excellence is such that they reflect the sunbeams like glass, and attract the attention of every observer.

The most perfect of these shining pavements lie at an elevation of about seven to eight thousand feet above the level of the sea, where the rock is close-grained, siliceous granite. Small fading patches may be found at from three to five thousand feet elevation on the driest and most enduring portions of vertical walls, where there is protection from the drip and friction of water; also, on compact swelling bosses partially protected by a covering of boulders.

On the north half of the Sierra the striated and polished surfaces are rarely found, not only because this portion of the chain is lower, but on account of the surface rocks being chiefly porous lavas subject to rapid waste. The moraines, also, though well preserved on the south half of the range, seem to be nearly wanting over a considerable portion of the north half, but the material of which they were composed is found in abundance, scattered and disintegrated, until its glacial origin is not obvious to the unskilled observer.

A similar blurred condition of the superficial records obtains throughout most of Oregon, Washington, British Columbia, and Alaska, due in great part to the action of excessive moisture. Even in southeastern Alaska, where the most extensive glaciers still exist, the more evanescent of the traces of their former greater extension, though comparatively recent, are more obscure than those of the ancient glaciers of California, where the climate is drier and the rocks more resisting. We are prepared, therefore, to find the finer lines of the glacial record dim or obliterated altogether in the Arctic regions, where the ground is mostly low and the action of frost and moisture specially destructive.

The Aleutian chain of islands sweeps westward in a regular curve, about a thousand miles long, from the Alaska Peninsula toward Kamchatka, nearly uniting the American and Asiatic continents. A very short geological time ago, just before the coming on of the glacial winter, the union of the two continents was probably complete. The entire chain appears to be simply a degraded portion of the North Pacific pre-glacial coast mountains, with its foot-hills and lowest portions of the connecting ridges between the peaks a few feet under water, the submerged ridges

Appendix

forming the passes between the islands as they exist today, while the broad plain to the north of the chain is now covered by the shallow waters of Bering Sea.

Now the evidence seems everywhere complete that this segregating degradation has been effected almost wholly by glacial action. Yet, strange to say, it is held by most observers who have made brief visits to different portions of the chain that each island is a distinct volcanic upheaval, but little changed since the period of emergence from the sea, an impression made no doubt by the volcanic character of most of the rocks, ancient and recent, of which they are composed, and by the many extinct or feebly active volcanoes occurring here and there along the summits of the highest masses. But, on the contrary, all the evidence we have seen goes to show that the amount of glacial denudation these rocks have undergone is very great, so great that, with the exception of the recent craters, almost every existing feature is distinctly glacial. The comparatively featureless pre-glacial rocks have been heavily sculptured and fashioned into the endless variety they now present of peak and ridge, valley and fiord and clustering islets, harmoniously correlated in accordance with glacial law.

On Mount Makushin,[1] whose summit reaches an elevation of about nine thousand feet above the sea, several small glaciers still exist, while others yet smaller may be hidden in the basins of other mountains not yet explored. The summit of Makushin, at the time my observations were made, was capped with heavy clouds, and from beneath these the glaciers were seen descending imposingly into the open sunshine to within a thousand or fifteen hundred feet of the sea level, the largest perhaps about six miles in length. After the clouds cleared away the summit was seen to be

[1]Muir probably adopted current estimates of the altitude of this volcano. Gannett's *Altitudes in Alaska* (1900) gives the elevation as 5474 feet, and the United States Coast and Geodetic Survey Map, No. 8860 (1916), as 5691 feet.

Appendix

heavily capped with ice, leaving only the crumbling edges of the dividing ridges and subordinate peaks free. The lower slopes of the mountain and the wide valleys proceeding from the glaciers present testimony of every kind to show that these glaciers now lingering on the summit once flowed directly into the sea. The adjacent mountains, though now mostly free from ice, are covered with glacial markings, extending over all the low grounds about their bases and the shores of the fiords, and over many of the rocks now under water. But besides this evidence of recent local glacial abundance, we find traces of far grander glacial conditions on the heavily abraded rocks along the shores of the passes separating the islands, and also in the low wide valleys extending in a direction parallel with the passes across the islands, indicating the movement of a vast ice-sheet from the north over the ground now covered by Bering Sea.

The amount of degradation this island region has undergone is only partially manifested by the crumbling, sharpened condition of the ridges and peaks, the abraded surfaces that have been overswept, and by the extent of the valleys and fiords, and the gaps between the mountains and islands.

That these valleys, fiords, forges, and gaps, great and small, like those of the Sierra, are not a result of local subsidences and upheavals, but of the removal of the material that once filled them, is shown by the broken condition and the similarity of the physical structure and composition of their contiguous sides, just as the correspondence between the tiers of masonry on either side of a broken gap in a wall shows that the missing blocks required to fill it up have been removed.

The chief agents of erosion and transportation are water and ice, each being regarded as the more influential by different observers, though the phenomena to which they give rise are widely different. All geologists recognize the fact that glaciers wear away the rocks over which they move, but great vagueness prevails as to the size of the fragments of erosion, and the way they are detached and removed; and if possible still greater vagueness prevails as to the forms and characteristics in general of the mountains, hills, rocks, valleys, etc., resulting from this erosion.

Towards the end of summer, when the snow is melted from the lower portions of the glaciers, particles of dust and sand may be seen scattered over their surfaces, together with angular masses of rocks, derived from the shattered storm-beaten cliffs above their fountains. The separation of these masses, which vary greatly in size, is due only in part to the action of the glacier, though they are all transported on its surface like floating drift on a river, and deposited together in moraines. The winds supply a portion of the sand and dust, some of the larger fragments are set free by the action of frost, rains, and general weathering agents, considerable quantities are swept down in avalanches of snow where the inclination of the slopes is favorable to their action, and shaken down by earthquake shocks, while the glacier itself plays an important part in the production of these superficial effects by undermining the cliffs from whence the fragments fall.

But in all moraines boulders and small dust particles may be recognized that have not been thus derived from the weathered cliffs and dividing ridges projecting above the glaciers, but from the rocks past which and over which the glaciers flow. The streams which drain glaciers are always turbid with finely ground mud particles worn off the bed-rocks by a sliding motion, accompanied by great pressure, giving rise to polished surfaces, and keeping up a waste that never for a moment ceases while the glacier exists; and besides these small particles boulders are found that may be traced to their origin in the bottoms or sides of the channels. Accordingly, an abrupt transition is discovered from the polished and plain portions of the channels to the more or less angular and fractured portions, showing that glaciers degrade the rocks over which they pass in at least two different ways, by grinding them into mud, and by crushing, breaking, and splitting them into a coarse detritus of chips and boulders, the forms and sizes of which are in great part determined by the divisional planes the rocks possess, and the intensity and direction of application of the force brought to bear on them. The quantity of this coarser material remaining in the channels along the lines of dispersal, and the probable rate of movement of the glaciers that quarried and transported it, form data from which some approximation to the rate of this method of degradation may be reached.

The amount of influence exerted on the Aleutian region by running water in its various forms, and by the winds, avalanches, and the atmosphere in degrading and fashioning the surface subsequent to the melting of the ice, is as yet scarcely more appreciable than it is in the upper middle portion of the Sierra; for, besides being much feebler in their action, the time during which the region has been exposed to their influence is comparatively short.

On the other hand, the quantity of material quarried and carried away by the force of ice, in the process of bringing the region into its present condition, can hardly be overestimated; for, with the exception of the recent volcanic cones, almost every noticeable feature, great and small, has evidently been ground down into the form of greatest strength in relation to the stress of oversweeping floods of ice. And that these present features are not the pre-glacial features merely smoothed and polished and otherwise superficially altered, but an entirely new set sculptured from a surface comparatively featureless, is manifested by the relationship existing between the spaces that separate them and the glacier fountains. The greater the valley or hollow of any sort, the greater the snow-collecting basin above it whence flowed the ice that created it, not a fiord or valley being found here or on any portion of the Pacific coast that does not conduct to fountains of vanished or residual glaciers corresponding with it in size and position as cause and effect.

And, furthermore, that the courses of the present valleys were not determined by the streams of water now occupying them, nor by pre-glacial streams, but by the glaciers of the last or of some former glacial period, is shown by the fact that the directions of the trends of all these valleys, however variable, are resultants of the forces of the main trunk glaciers that filled them and their inflowing tributary glaciers, the wriggling fortuitous trends of valleys formed by the action of water being essentially different from those formed by ice; and therefore not liable to be confounded with them. Neither can we suppose pre-existing fissures or local subsidences to have exercised any primary determining influence, there being no conceivable coincidence between the trends of fissures and subsidences and the specific trends of ice-created valleys and basins in general, nor between the position and direction of extension of these hypothetical fissures, subsidences, and foldings and the positions of ice-fountains.

The Pribilof Islands, St. Paul, St. George, Walrus, and Otter, appear in general views from the sea as mere storm-beaten remnants of a once continuous land, wasted into bluffs around their shores by the action of the waves, all their upper surfaces being planed down by a heavy over-sweeping ice-sheet, slightly roughened here and there with low ridges and hillocks that alternate with shallow valleys. None of their features, as far as I could discover without opportunity for close observation, showed any trace of local glaciation or of volcanic action subsequent to the period of universal glaciation.

St. Lawrence Island, the largest in Bering Sea, is situated at a distance of about one hundred and twenty miles off the mouths of the Yukon, and forty miles from the nearest point on the coast of Siberia. It is about a hundred miles long from east to west, fifteen miles in average width, and is chiefly composed of various kinds of granite, slate, and lava.

The highest portion along the middle is diversified with groups of volcanic cones, some of which are of considerable size and clearly post-glacial in age, presenting well-defined craters and regular slopes down to the base, though I saw no evidence of their having poured forth extensive streams of molten lava over the adjacent rocks since the close of the glacial period; for, with the exception of the ground occupied by the cones, all the surface is marked with glacial inscriptions of the most telling kind—moraines, erratic boulders, *roches moutonnées*, in great abundance and variety as to size, and alternating ridges and valleys with wide U-shaped cross-sections, and with nearly parallel trends across the island in a general north to south direction, some of them extending from shore to shore, and all showing subordination to the grinding, furrowing action of a broad oversweeping ice-sheet.

Some of the widest gap-like valleys have been eroded nearly to the level of the sea, indicating that if the ice action had gone on much longer the present single island would have been eroded into a group of small ones; or the entire mass of the island would have been degraded beneath the sea level, obliterating it from the landscape to be in part restored perhaps by the antagonistic elevating volcanic action. The action of local glaciers has been comparatively light hereabouts, not enough greatly to obscure or interrupt the overmastering effects of the ice-sheet, though they have given marked character to the sculpture of some of the higher portions of the island.

The two Diomede Islands and Fairway Rock are mostly residual masses of granite brought into relief and separated from one another and from the general mass of the continent, by the action of ice in removing the missing material, while the islands remain because of superior resistance offered to the universal degrading force. That they are remnants of a once continuous land now separated by Bering Strait is indicated by the relative condition of the sides of the islands and of the contiguous shoulders of the continents, East Cape and Cape Prince of Wales, while the general configuration of the islands shows that they have been subjected to a glaciation of the most comprehensive kind, leaving them as *roches moutonnées* on a grand scale.

I discovered traces of local glaciation on the largest of the three, but the effects produced by this cause are comparatively slight, while the action of excessive moisture in the form of almost constant fogs and rains throughout the summer months, combined with frost and thaw, has effected a considerable amount of denudation, manifested by groups of crumbling pinnacles occurring here and there on the summits.

Sledge, King, and Herald Islands are evidently of similar origin, displaying the same glacial traces, and varying chiefly in the amount of post-glacial waste they have suffered, and in the consequent degree of clearness of the testimony they present. During our visit to Herald Island an exceptionally favorable opportunity offered as to the time of year, state of the weather, etc., for observation.

Kellett, who first discovered this island and landed on it under adverse circumstances, describes it as an inaccessible rock. The sides are indeed precipitous in the main, but mountaineers would find many slopes and gullies by which the summit could be easily attained. We landed on the southwest side, opposite the mouth of a small valley, the bed of a vanished glacier. A short gully which conducts from the water's edge to the mouth of the valley proper is very steep, and at the time of our visit was blocked with compacted snow, in which steps had to be cut, but beyond this no difficulty was encountered, the ice having graded a fine broad way to the summit. Thence following the highest ground nearly to the northwestern extremity, we obtained views of most of the surface. The highest point is about twelve hundred feet above the sea, about a mile and a half from the northwest end of the island, and four and a half miles from the southeast. This makes the island about six miles long, the average width being about two miles.

Near the middle of the island there is a low gap, where the width is only about half a mile, and the height of the summit of this portion of the water-shed between the two sides is only about two hundred and fifty feet. The entire island as far as seen is a mass of granite, with the exception of a patch of metamorphic slates near the middle, which no doubt owes its existence, with so considerable a height, to the superior resistance it

Appendix

offered to the degrading action of ice, traces of which are presented in the general *moutonnée* form of the island, and in the smooth parallel ridges and valleys trending north and south. These evidently have not been determined as to size, form, position, or the direction of their trends by subsidences, upheavals, foldings, or any structural peculiarity of the rocks in which they have been eroded, but simply by the mechanical force of an oversweeping ice-sheet.

The effects of local glaciers are seen in short valleys of considerable depth as compared with the area from which their fountain snows were derived. We noticed four of these valleys that had been occupied by residual glaciers; and on the hardest and most enduring of the upswelling rock bosses several patches of the ancient scored and polished surface were discovered, still in a good state of preservation. That these local glaciers have but recently vanished is indicated by the raw appearance of the surface of their beds, while one small glacier remnant occupying a sheltered hollow and possessing a well-characterized terminal moraine seems to be still feebly active in the last stage of decadence. This small granite island, standing solitary in the Polar Ocean, we regard as one of the most interesting and significant of the monuments of geographical change effected by general glaciation.

Our stay on Wrangell Land was too short to admit of more than a hasty examination of a few square miles of surface near the eastern extremity. The rock here is a close-grained clay slate, cleaving freely into thin flakes, with occasional compact metamorphic masses rising above the general surface or forming cliffs along the shore. The soil about the banks of a river of considerable size, that enters the ocean here, has evidently been derived in the main from the underlying slates, indicating a rapid weathering of the surface. A few small deposits of moraine material were discovered containing traveled boulders of quartz and granite, no doubt from the mountains in which the river takes its rise, while the valley now occupied by the river manifests its glacial origin in its form and trends, the small portion in the middle eroded by the river itself being clearly distinguished by its abrupt angular sides, which contrast sharply with the glacial outlines.

In general views obtained in sailing along its southern coast the phenomena presented seemed essentially the same as have been described elsewhere—hills, valleys, and sculptured peaks, testifying in all their main trends and contours to the action of ice. A range of mountains of moderate height extends from one extremity of the island to the other, a distance of about sixty-five miles, the highest point as measured by Lieutenant Berry being twenty-five hundred feet above the sea.

All the coast region of Siberia that came under our observation, from the Gulf of Anadir to North Cape, presents traces in great abundance and variety of universal as well as local glaciation. Between Plover and St. Lawrence Bays, where the mountains attain their greatest elevation and where local glaciation has been heaviest, the coast is lacerated with deep fiords, on the lofty granite walls of which the glacial records are in many places well preserved, and offer evidence that could hardly be overlooked by the most careless observer.

Our first general views of this region were obtained on June 7, when it was yet winter, and the landscape was covered with snow down to the water's edge. After several days of storm the clouds lifted, exposing the heavily abraded fronts of outstanding cliffs; then the smooth overswept ridges and slopes at the base of the mountains came in sight, and one angular peak after another, until a continuous range forty to fifty miles long could be seen from one standpoint. Many of the peaks are fluted with the narrow channels of avalanches, and hollowed with *névé* amphitheaters of great beauty of form, while long withdrawing fiords and valleys may be traced back into the recesses of the highest groups, once the beds of glaciers that flowed in imposing ranks to the sea.

Plover Bay, which I examined in detail, may be taken as a good representative of the fiords of this portion of the coast. The walls rise to an average height of about two thousand feet, and present a severely desolate and bedraggled appearance, owing to the crumbling condition of the rocks, which in most places are being rapidly disintegrated, loading the slopes with loose, shifting detritus whenever the angle is low enough to allow it to come to rest. When examined closely, however, this loose material is found to be of no great depth. The solid rock comes to the surface in many places, and on the most enduring portions rounded glaciated surfaces are still found grooved, scratched, and polished in small patches from the sea-level up to a height of a thousand feet or more.

Large taluses with their bases under the water occur on both sides of the fiord in front of the side cañons that partially separate the main mountain masses that form the walls. These taluses are composed in great part of moraine material, brought down by avalanches of snow from the terminal moraines of small vanished glaciers that lay at a height of from one to five thousand feet, in recesses where the snow accumulated from the surrounding slopes, and where sheltered from the direct action of the sun the glaciers lingered longest. These recent moraines are formed of several concentric masses shoved together, showing that the glaciers to which they belonged melted and receded gradually with slight fluctuations of level and rate of decadence, in accordance with conditions of snow-fall, temperature, etc., like those of lower latitudes.

When the main central glacier that filled this fiord was in its prime as a distinct glacier it measured about thirty miles in length and from five to six miles in width, and was from two to three thousand feet in depth. It then had at least five main tributaries, which, as the trunk melted, became independent glaciers; and, again, as the trunks of these main tributaries melted, their smaller tributaries, numbering about seventy-five, and from less than a mile to several miles in length, became separate glaciers and lingered probably for centuries in the high, cool fountains. These also, as far as we have seen, have vanished, though possibly some wasting remnant may still exist in the highest and best-protected recesses about the head of the fiord.

Appendix

Along the coast, a distance of fifteen or twenty miles to the eastward and southward of the mouth of Metchigme Bay, interesting deposits occur of roughly stratified glacial detritus in the form of sand, gravel and boulders. They rise from the shore in raw, wave-washed bluffs about forty feet high and extend to the base of the mountains as a gently inclined plain, with a width in some places of two or three miles. Similar morainal deposits were also observed on the American coast at Golofnin Bay, Kotzebue Sound, Cape Prince of Wales, and elsewhere. At Cape Prince of Wales the formation rises in successive well-defined terraces.

The peninsula, the extremity of which forms East Cape, trends nearly in an easterly direction from the mainland, and consequently occupies a telling position with reference to ice moving from the northward. I was therefore eager to examine it to see what testimony it might have to offer. We landed during favorable weather on the south side at a small Eskimo village built on a rough moraine, and pushed on direct to the summit of the watershed, from which good general views of nearly all the surface of the peninsula were obtained.

The dividing ridge along the high eastern portion is traversed by a telling series of parallel grooves and small valleys trending north and south approximately, the curves on the north commencing nearly at the water's edge, while the south side is more or less precipitous. The culminating point of the elevated eastern portion of the peninsula is about twenty-five hundred feet high, and has been cut from the mainland and added as another island to the Diomede group, the wide gap of low ground connecting it with the adjacent mountainous portion of the mainland being only a few feet above tide-water. Out in the midst of this low, flat region smooth upswelling *roches moutonnées* were discovered here and there like groups of small islands, with trends and contours emphatically glacial, all telling the action of a universal abrading ice-sheet moving southward.

Hence along the coast to Cape North, which is the limit of our observations in this direction, the same class of ice phenomena was discovered—moraine material, washed and re-formed, *moutonnée* masses of the harder rocks standing like islands in the low, mossy tundra, and traveled boulders and pebbles lying stranded on the summits of rocky headlands.

These enduring monuments are particularly abundant and significant in the neighborhood of Cape Wankarem, where the granite is more compact and resisting than is commonly found in the Arctic regions we have visited, and consequently has longer retained the more evanescent of the glacial markings. Cape Wankarem is a narrow, flat-topped, residual mass of this enduring granite, on the summit of which two patches of the original polished surface were discovered that still retains the fine striae and many erratic boulders of slate, quartz, and various kinds of lava, which, from the configuration and geographical position of the cape with reference to the surrounding region, could not have been brought to their present resting-places by any local glacier.

Cape Serdzakamen is another of these residual island masses, brought into relief by general glacial denudation, manifesting its origin in every feature, and corroborating the testimony given at Cape Wankarem and elsewhere in the most emphatic manner.

All the sections of the tundra seen either on the Siberian or Alaskan coast lead towards the conclusion that the ground is glacial, re-formed under the action of running water derived in broad, shallow currents from the melting, receding edge of the ice-sheet, and also in some measure from ice left on the high lands after the main ice-sheet had been withdrawn; for these low, flat deposits differ in no particular of form or composition that we have been able to detect from those still in process of formation in front of the large receding glaciers of southeastern Alaska. On many of the so-called "mud-flats" extending from the snouts of glaciers that have receded a few miles from the shore, mosses and lichens and other kinds of tundra vegetation are being gradually acquired, and when thus clothed these patches of tundra are not to be distinguished from the extensive deposits about the shores of the Arctic regions.

Appendix

The phenomena observed on the American coast from St. Michael to Point Barrow differ in no essential particular from those which have been described on the opposite shores of Siberia. Moraines more or less wasted, and re-formations of moraine material, smooth overswept ridges with glacial trends and the corresponding valleys, *roches moutonnées*, and the fountain amphitheaters of local glaciers were observed almost everywhere on the mountainous portions of the coast, though in general more deeply weathered, owing mainly to the occurrence of less resisting rocks, limestones, sandstones, porous lavas, etc.

A number of well-characterized moraines so situated with reference to topographical conditions as to have escaped destructive washing were noticed near Cape Lisburne, and moraine deposits of great extent at Kotzebue Sound and Golofnin Bay, of which many fine sections were exposed. At the latter locality, judging from the comparatively fresh appearance of the rock surfaces and deposits around the head of the bay, and the height and extent of the ice-fountains, the glacier that discharged here was probably the last to vanish from the American shore of Bering Sea.

As to the thickness attained by the ice-sheet over the regions that we have been examining during the period of greatest glacial development, we have seen that it passed heavily over the islands of Bering Sea and the adjacent mountains on either side, especially at East Cape and Cape Prince of Wales, at a height of twenty-five hundred feet or more above the bottom of Bering Sea and Strait, the average depth of water here being about a hundred and fifty feet. And though the lowest portion of the land beneath the ice may have been degraded to a considerable depth subsequent to the time when these highest portions were left bare, on the other hand the level of the ice must have been considerably higher than the summits over which it passed, inasmuch as they give evidence of having been heavily abraded. It appears, therefore, that the thickness of the general northern ice-sheet throughout a considerable portion of its history was not less than twenty-five hundred feet, and probably more, over the northern portion of the region now covered by Bering Sea and part of the Arctic Ocean.

In view of this colossal ice-flood grinding on throughout the hundreds of thousands of years of the glacial period, the excavation of the shallow basins of Bering Sea and Strait and the Arctic Ocean must be taken as only a small part of the erosion effected; for so shallow are these waters, were the tallest sequoias planted on the bottom where soundings have been made, their tops would rise in most places a hundred feet or more above the surface. The Plover Bay glacier, as we have shown, eroded the granite in the formation of its channel to a depth of not less than two thousand feet, and the amount of erosion effected by the ice-sheet was probably much greater.

It appears, therefore, in summing up the results of our observations along the North Pacific and Arctic coasts:—

1. That the southernmost glacier lies on the Sierra near latitude 36°; the northernmost, with perhaps a few exceptions, near 62°.
2. That the region of greatest glaciation lies between 56° and 61°, where the mountains are highest and the snowfall greatest.
3. That an ice-sheet flowed from the Arctic regions, from beyond the end of the continent, pursuing a general southerly direction, and discharged into the Pacific Ocean south of the Aleutian Islands.
4. That of this continuous ice-sheet, extending from the Arctic Ocean beyond the northern extremity of the continent, the glaciers, great and small, now existing are the remnants.
5. That the basins of Bering Sea and Strait and of the adjacent portion of the Arctic Ocean are simply those portions of the bed of the ice-sheet which were eroded to a moderate depth beneath the level of the sea, and over which the ocean waters were gradually extended as the ice-sheet was withdrawn, thus separating the continents of Asia and America, at the close of the glacial period.

Appendix

We are now better prepared to read the changes that have taken place on the Sierra, and fortunately, as we have already seen, nowhere is the glacial record clearer.

II
Botanical Notes

INTRODUCTORY

The plants named in the following notes were collected at many localities on the coasts of Alaska and Siberia, and on St. Lawrence, Wrangell, and Herald Islands, between about latitude 54° and 71° N., longitude 161° and 178° W., in the course of short excursions, some of them less than an hour in length. Inasmuch as the flora of the arctic and subarctic regions is nearly the same everywhere, the discovery of many species new to science was not to be expected. The collection, however, will no doubt be valuable for comparison with the plants of other regions. In general the physiognomy of the vegetation of the polar regions resembles that of the alpine valleys of the temperate zones; so much so that the botanist on the coast of Arctic Siberia or America might readily fancy himself on the Sierra Nevada at a height of ten to twelve thousand feet above the sea.

There is no line of perpetual snow on any portion of the Arctic regions known to explorers. The snow disappears every summer, not only from the low, sandy shores and boggy tundras, but also from the tops of the mountains, and all the upper slopes and valleys with the exception of small patches of drifts and avalanche-heaps hardly noticeable in general views. But though nowhere excessively deep or permanent, the snow-mantle is universal during winter, and the plants are solidly frozen and buried for nearly three fourths of the year. In this condition they enjoy a sleep and rest about as profound as death, from which they awake in the months of June and July in vigorous health, and speedily reach a far higher development of leaf and flower and fruit than is generally supposed. On the drier banks and hills about Kotzebue Sound, Cape Thompson, and Cape Lisburne, many species show but little climatic repression, and during the long summer days grow tall enough to wave in the wind, and unfold flowers in as rich profusion and as highly colored as may be found in regions lying a thousand miles farther south.

To the botanist approaching any portion of the Aleutian chain of islands from the southward during the winter or spring months, the view is severely desolate and forbidding. The snow comes down to the water's edge in solid white, interrupted only by dark, outstanding bluffs with faces too steep for snow to lie on, and by the backs of rounded rocks and long, rugged reefs beaten and overswept by heavy breakers rolling in from the Pacific, while throughout nearly every month of the year the higher mountains are wrapped in gloomy, dripping storm-clouds.

Nevertheless, vegetation here is remarkably close and luxuriant, and crowded with showy bloom, covering almost every foot of the ground up to a height of about a thousand feet above the sea—the harsh trachytic rocks, and even the cindery bases of the craters, as well as the moraines and rough soil-beds outspread on the low portions of the short, narrow valleys.

On the twentieth of May we found the showy *Geum glaciale* already in flower, also an arctostaphylos and draba, on a slope facing the south, near the harbor of Unalaska. The willows, too, were then beginning to put forth their catkins, while a multitude of green points were springing up in sheltered spots wherever the snow had vanished. At a height of four or five hundred feet, however, winter was still unbroken, with scarce a memory of the rich bloom of summer.

During a few short excursions along the shores of Unalaska Harbor, and on two of the adjacent mountains, towards the end of May and the beginning of October, we saw about fifty species of flowering plants—empetrum, vaccinium, bryanthus, pyrola, arctostaphylos, ledum, cassiope, lupinus, geranium, epilobium, silene, draba, and saxifraga, being the most telling and characteristic of the genera represented. *Empetrum nigrum*, a bryanthus, and three species of vaccinium make a grand display when in flower, and show their massed colors at a considerable distance.

Almost the entire surface of the valleys and hills and lower slopes of the mountains is covered with a dense, spongy plush of lichens and mosses similar to that which covers the tundras of the Arctic regions, making a rich green mantle on which the showy, flowering plants are strikingly relieved, though these grow far more luxuriantly on the banks of the streams where the drainage is less interrupted. Here also the ferns, of which I saw three species, are taller and more abundant, some of them arching their broad, delicate fronds over one's shoulders, while in similar situations the tallest of the five grasses that were seen reaches a height of nearly six feet, and forms a growth close enough for the farmer's scythe.

Not a single tree has been seen on any of the islands of the chain west of Kodiak, excepting a few spruces brought from Sitka and planted at Unalaska by the Russians about fifty years ago. They are still alive in a dwarfed condition, having made scarce any appreciable growth since they were planted. These facts are the more remarkable, since in southeastern Alaska, lying both to the north and south of here, and on the many islands of the Alexander Archipelago, as well as on the mainland, forests of beautiful conifers flourish exuberantly and attain noble dimensions, while the climatic conditions generally do not appear to differ greatly from those that obtain on these treeless islands.

Wherever cattle have been introduced they have prospered and grown fat on the abundance of rich nutritious pasturage to be found almost everywhere in the deep, withdrawing valleys and on the green slopes of the hills and mountains, but the wetness of the summer months will always prevent the making of hay in any considerable quantities.

The agricultural possibilities of these islands seem also to be very

Appendix

limited. The hardier of the cereals—rye, barley, and oats—make a good, vigorous growth, and head out, but seldom or never mature, on account of insufficient sunshine and overabundance of moisture in the form of long-continued, drizzling fogs and rains. Green crops, however, as potatoes, turnips, cabbages, beets, and most other common garden vegetables, thrive wherever the ground is thoroughly drained and has a southerly exposure.

ST. LAWRENCE ISLAND

St. Lawrence Island, as far as our observations extended, is mostly a dreary mass of granite and lava of various forms and colors, roughened with volcanic cones, covered with snow, and rigidly bound in ocean ice for half the year. Inasmuch as it lies broadsidewise to the direction pursued by the great ice-sheet that recently filled Bering Sea, and its rocks offered unequal resistance to the denuding action of the ice, the island is traversed by numerous ridges and low, gap-like valleys all trending in the same general direction. Some of the lowest of these transverse valleys have been degraded nearly to the level of the sea, showing that if the glaciation to which the island has been subjected had been slightly greater, we should have found several islands here instead of one.

At the time of our first visit, May 28, winter still had full possession, but eleven days later we found the dwarf willows, drabas, erigerons, and saxifrages pushing up their buds and leaves, on spots bare of snow, with wonderful rapidity. This was the beginning of spring at the northwest end of the island. On July 4 the flora seemed to have reached its highest development. The bottoms of the glacial valleys were in many places covered with tall grasses and carices evenly planted and forming meadows of considerable size, while the drier portions and the sloping grounds about them were enlivened with gay, highly colored flowers from an inch to nearly two feet in height, such as *Aconitum Napellus*, L., var. *delphinifolium*, Ser., *Polemonium cœruleum*, L., *Papaver nudicaule*, L., *Draba alpina*, L., and *Silene acaulis*, L., in large, closely flowered tufts, as well as andromeda, ledum, linnæa, cassiope, and several species of vaccinium and saxifraga.

ST. MICHAEL

The region about St. Michael is a magnificent tundra, crowded with Arctic lichens and mosses, which here develop under most favorable conditions. In the spongy plush formed by the lower plants, in which one sinks almost knee-deep at every step, there is a sparse growth of grasses, carices, and rushes, tall enough to wave in the wind, while empetrum, the dwarf birch, and the various heathworts flourish here in all their beauty of bright leaves and flowers. The moss mantle for the most part rests on a stratum of ice that never melts to any great extent, and the ice on a bed rock of black vesicular lava. Ridges of the lava rise here and there above the general level in rough masses, affording ground for plants that like a drier soil. Numerous hollows and watercourses also occur on the general tundra, whose well-drained banks are decked with gay flowers in lavish abundance, and meadow patches of grasses shoulder-high, suggestive of regions much farther south.

The following plants and a few doubtful species not yet determined were collected here:

Aspidium fragrans, Sw.
Woodsia ilvensis, (L.), R. Br.
Eriophorum capitatum, Hos.
Carex vulgaris, (Fries), Willd.,
    var. *alpina*.
Lloydia serotina, (Sweet),
    Reichenb.
Tofieldia coccinea, Richards.
Betula nana, L.

Alnus viridis, DC.
Polygonum alpinum, All.
Arenaria lateriflora, L.
Stellaria longipes, Goldie.
Silene acaulis, L.
Anemone narcissiflora, L.
Anemone parviflora, Michx.
Caltha palustris, L., var.
    asarifolia, Rothr.

Appendix

Corydalis pauciflora.
Draba alpina, L.
Draba incana, L.
Eutrema arenicola, Richards.
Saxifraga nivalis, L.
Saxifraga hieracifolia, Waldst. &
    Kit.
Rubus Chamæmorus, L.
Rubus arcticus, L.
Potentilla nivea, L.
Dryas octopetala, L.
Oxytropis podocarpa, Gray.
Astragalus alpinus, L.
Astragalus frigidus, Gray, var.
    littoralis.
Lathyrus maritimus, Bigel.
Epilobium latifolium, L.
Cassiope tetragone, (D. Don.),
    Desv.
Andromeda polifolia, L.
Loiseleuria procumbens, Desv.
Vaccinium Vitis-Idæa, L.

Arctostaphylos alpina, Spreng.
Ledum palustre, L.
Diapensia lapponica, L.
Armeria vulgaris, Willd.
Primula borealis, Duby.
Polemonium cœruleum, L.
Mertensia paniculata, Desv.
Pedicularis sudetica, Willd.
Pedicularis euphrasioides, Stev.
Pedicularis Langsdorffi, Fisch.,
    var. lanata, Gray.
Pinguicula villosa, L.
Linnæa borealis, Gronov.
Valeriana capitata, (Pall.),
    Willd.
Saussurea alpina, DC.
Nardosmia frigida, Hook.
Senecio frigidus, Less.
Senecio palustris, Hook.
Arnica angustifolia, Vahl.
Artemisia arctica, Bess.
Matricaria inodora, L.

GOLOFNIN BAY

The tundra flora on the west side of Golofnin Bay is remarkably close and luxuriant, covering almost every foot of the ground, the hills as well as the valleys, while the sandy beach and a bank of coarsely stratified moraine material a few yards back from the beach were blooming like a garden with *Lathyrus maritimus, Iris sibirica, Polemonium cœruleum,* etc., diversified with clumps and patches of *Elymus arenarius, Alnus viridis,* and *Abies alba.*

Appendix

This is one of the few points on the east side of Bering Sea where trees closely approach the shore. The white spruce occurs here in small groves or thickets of well-developed, erect trees fifteen or twenty feet high, near the level of the sea, at a distance of about six or eight miles from the mouth of the bay, and gradually becomes irregular and dwarfed as it approaches the shore. Here a number of dead and dying specimens were observed, indicating that conditions of soil, climate, and relations to other plants were becoming more unfavorable, and causing the tree-line to recede from the coast.

The following collection was made here July 10:

Aspidium spinulosum, Sw.
Elymus arenarius, L.
Poa trivialis, L.
Carex vesicaria, L., var. *alpigena*, Fries.
Lloydia serotina, (Sweet), Reichenb.
Iris sibirica, L.
Arenaria peploides, L.
Eutrema arenicola, Hook.
Spiræa betulifolia, Pall.

Rubus arcticus, L.
Epilobium latifolium, L.
Vaccinium Vitis-Idæa, L.
Trientalis europæa, L., var. *arctica*, Ledeb.
Gentiana glauca, Pall.
Polemonium cœruleum, L.
Pinguicula villosa, L.
Chrysanthemum arcticum, L.
Artemisia Tilesii, Ledeb.

KOTZEBUE SOUND

The flora of the region about the head of Kotzebue Sound is hardly less luxuriant and rich in species than that of other points, visited by the Corwin, lying several degrees farther south. Fine nutritious grasses suitable for the fattening of cattle, and from two to six feet high, are not of rare occurrence on meadows of considerable extent, and along streambanks wherever the stagnant waters of the tundra have been drained off, while in similar localities the most showy of the arctic plants bloom in all their freshness and beauty, manifesting no sign of frost, or unfavorable conditions of any kind whatever.

A striking result of the airing and draining of the boggy tundra soil is shown on the ice-bluffs around Eschscholtz Bay, where it has been undermined by the melting of the ice on which it rests. In falling down the face of the ice-wall it is well shaken and rolled before it again comes to rest on terraced or gently sloping portions of the wall. The original vegetation of the tundra is thus destroyed, and tall grasses spring up on the fresh, mellow ground as it accumulates from time to time, growing lush and rank, though in many places that we noted these new soil-beds are not more than a foot in depth, and lie on the solid ice.

At the time of our last visit to this interesting region, about the middle of September, the weather was still fine, suggesting the Indian summer of the Western States. The tundra glowed in the mellow sunshine with the colors of the ripe foliage of vaccinium, empetrum, arctostaphylos, and dwarf birch; red, purple, and yellow, in pure bright tones, while the berries, hardly less beautiful, were scattered everywhere as if they had been sown broadcast with a lavish hand, the whole blending harmoniously with the neutral tints of the furred bed of lichens and mosses on which the bright leaves and berries were painted.

On several points about the sound the white spruce occurs in small, compact groves within a few miles of the shore; and pyrola, which belongs to wooded regions, is abundant where no trees are now in sight, tending to show that areas of considerable extent, now treeless, were once forested.

The plants collected are:

Luzula hyperborea, R. Br.
Allium schœnoprasum, L.
Salix polaris, Wahlenb.
Polygonum viviparum, L.
Stellaria longipes, Goldie.

Cerastium alpinum, L., var.
   Behringianum, Regel.
Papaver nudicaule, L.
Saxifraga tricuspidata, Retz.
Potentilla anserina, L., var.

Appendix

Potentilla biflora, Willd.
Potentilla fruticosa, L.
Lupinus arcticus, Watson.
Hedysarum boreale, Nutt.
Empetrum nigrum, L.
Pyrola rotundifolia, L., var.
  pumila, Hook.
Arctostaphylos alpina,
  Spreng.
Cassiope tetragone, (D. Don),
  Desv.
Ledum palustre, L.
Vaccinium Vitis-Idœa, L.

Vaccinium uliginosum, L., var.
  mucronata, Herder.
Armeria vulgaris, Willd., var.
  arctica, Cham.
Trientalis europœa, L., var.
  arctica, Ledeb.
Mertensia maritima, L. (S. F.
  Gray), Desv.
Castilleia pallida, Kunth.
Pedicularis sudetica, Willd.
Pedicularis verticillata, L.
Galium boreale, L.
Senecio palustris, Hook.

CAPE THOMPSON

The Cape Thompson flora is richer in species and individuals than that of any other point on the Arctic shores we have seen, owing no doubt mainly to the better drainage of the ground through the fissured frost-cracked limestone, which hereabouts is the principal rock.

Where the hill-slopes are steepest the rock frequently occurs in loose, angular masses, and is entirely bare of soil. but between these barren slopes there are valleys where the showiest of the arctic plants bloom in rich profusion and variety, forming brilliant masses of color—purple, yellow, and blue—where certain species form beds of considerable size, almost to the exclusion of others.

The following list was obtained here July 19:

Cystopteris fragilis, (L.), Bernh.
Trisetum subspicatum, Beauv.,
  var. molle, Gray.
Glyceria —

Festuca sativa (?) [F. ovina, L.?]
Carex rariflora, Wahlenb.
Carex vulgaris, Fries, var. alpina,
  (C. rigida, Good.)

[213]

Appendix

Salix polaris, Wahlenb., and two
   other species undetermined.
Polygonum Bistorta, L.
Rumex crispus, L.
Cerastium alpinum, L., var.
   Behringianum, Regel.
Silene acaulis, L.
Arenaria verna, L., var. rubella,
   Hook. f.
Arenaria arctica, Stev.
Stellaria longipes, Goldie.
Anemone narcissiflora, L.
Anemone multifida, Poir.
Anemone parviflora, Michx.
Anemone parviflora, Michx.,
   variety.
Ranunculus affinis, R. Br.
Caltha asarifolia, DC.
Papaver nudicaule, L.
Draba stellata, Jacq., var. nivalis,
   Regel.
Draba incana, L.
Cardamine pratensis, L.
Cheiranthus pygmæus, Adams.
Pedicularis capitata, Adams
Geum glaciale, Fisch.
Nardosmia corymbosa, Hook.
Erigeron Muirii, Gray, n. sp.
Parrya nudicaulis, (Boiss.), Regel,
   var. aspera, Regel.
Boykinia Richardsoni, Gray.
Saxifraga tricuspidata, Retz.

Saxifraga cernua, L.
Saxifraga flagellaris, Willd.
Saxifraga davurica, Willd.
Saxifraga punctata, L.
Saxifraga nivalis, L.
Dryas octopetala, L.
Potentilla biflora, Willd.
Potentilla nivea, L.
Hedysarum boreale, Nutt.
Oxytropis podocarpa, Gray.
Epilobium latifolium, L.
Cassiope tetragone, (D. Don.),
   Desv.
Vaccinium uliginosum, L., var.
   mucronata, Herder.
Vaccinium Vitis-Idæa, L.
Dodecatheon Meadia, L., var.
   frigidum, Gray.
Androsace chamæjasme, Willd.
Phlox sibirica, L.
Polemonium humile, Willd.
Polemonium cœruleum, L.
Myosotis sylvatica, var. alpestris,
   Hoffm.
Eritrichium nanum, Schrad., var.
   arctioides.
Taraxacum palustre, DC.
Senecio frigidus, Less.
Artemisia glomerata, Ledeb.
Artemisia tomentosa [tomentella,
   Trautv.?]

Appendix

At Cape Prince of Wales we obtained:

Tofieldia coccinea, Richards.
Loiseleuria procumbens, Desv.
Andromeda polifolia, L., *forma arctica*.

Vaccinium Vitis-Idæa, L.
Armeria arctica, (Wallr.), Stev.
Androsace chamæjasme, Willd.
Taraxacum palustre, DC.

TWENTY MILES EAST OF CAPE LISBURNE

Lychnis apetala, L.
Anemone narcissiflora, L., var.
Draba hirta, L.
Saxifraga Eschscholtzii, Sternb.
Saxifraga flagellaris, Willd.
Chrysosplenium alternifolium, L.
Potentilla nivea, L.
Potentilla biflora, Willd.

Oxytropis campestris, DC.
Primula borealis, Duby.
Androsace chamæjasme, Willd.
Phlox sibirica, L.
Geum glaciale, Fisch.
Erigeron uniflorus, L.
Artemisia glomerata, Ledeb.

CAPE WANKAREM, SIBERIA

Near Cape Wankarem, August 7 and 8, we collected:

Elymus arenarius, L.
Alopecurus alpinus, Sm.
Poa arctica, R. Br.
Calamagrostis deschampsioides, Trin.
Luzula hyperborea, R. Br.

Luzula spicata, (DC.), Desv.
Lychnis apetala, L.
Claytonia virginica, L.
Ranunculus pygmæus, Wahlenb.
Chrysosplenium alternifolium, L.
Saxifraga cernua, L.

[215]

Appendix

Saxifraga stellaris, L., var. comosa
Saxifraga rivularis, L., var.
    hyperborea, Hook.
Polemonium cœruleum, L.
Pedicularis Langsdorffi, Fisch.

Nardosmia frigida, Hook.
Chrysanthemum arcticum, L.
Senecio frigidus, Less.
Artemisia vulgaris, var. Tilesii,
    Ledeb.

PLOVER BAY, SIBERIA

The mountains bounding the glacial fiord called Plover Bay, though beautiful in their combinations of curves and peaks as they are seen touching each other delicately and rising in bold, picturesque groups, are nevertheless severely desolate-looking from the absence of trees and large shrubs, and indeed of vegetation of any kind dense enough to give color in telling quantities, or to soften the harsh rockiness of the steepest portions of the walls. Even the valleys opening back from the water here and there on either side are mostly bare as seen at a distance of a mile or two, and show only a faint tinge of green, derived from dwarf willows, heathworts, and sedges chiefly.

The most interesting of the plants found here are *Rhododendron kamtschaticum*, Pall., and the handsome blue-flowered *Saxifraga oppositifolia*, L., both of which are abundant.

The following were collected July 12 and August 26:

Arenaria macrocarpa, Pursh.
Aconitum Napellus, L., var.
    delphinifolium, Ser.
Anemone narcissiflora, L.
Draba alpina, L.
Parrya Ermanni, Ledeb.
Saxifraga oppositifolia, L.
Saxifraga punctata, L.
Saxifraga cæspitosa, L.

Dryas octopetala, L.
Oxytropis podocarpa, Gray.
Rhododendron kamtschaticum,
    Pall.
Cassiope tetragona, (D. Don.),
    Desv.
Diapensia lapponica, L.
Gentiana glauca, Pall.
Geum glaciale, Fisch.

Appendix

On Herald Island the common polar cryptogamous vegetation is well represented and developed. So also are the flowering plants, almost the entire surface of the island, with the exception of the sheer, crumbling bluffs along the shores, being quite tellingly dotted and tufted with characteristic species. The following list [1] was obtained:

Gymnandra Stelleri, Cham. & Schlecht.

Alopecurus alpinus, Sm.

Luzula hyperborea, R. Br.

Salix polaris, Wahlenb.

Stellaria longipes, Goldie, var. *Edwardsii*, T. & G.

Papaver nudicaule, L.

Draba alpina, L.

Saxifraga punctata, L.

Saxifraga serpyllifolia, Pursh.

Saxifraga sileniflora, (Hook.), Sternb.

Saxifraga bronchialis, L.

Saxifraga stellaris, L., var. *comosa*, Poir.

Saxifraga rivularis, L., var. *hyperborea*, Hook.

Saxifraga hieracifolia, Waldst. & Kit.

Potentilla frigida, Vill.?

Senecio frigidus, Less.

WRANGELL LAND

Our stay on the one point of Wrangell Land that we touched was far too short to admit of making anything like as full a collection of the plants of so interesting a region as was desirable. We found the rock formation where we landed and for some distance along the coast to the eastward

---

[1] Berthold Seemann, botanist of H. M. S. Herald in 1849, reported the finding of eight plants on a width of thirty feet of shore, which, he says, "was the whole extent we had to walk over." The plants were the following: *Artemisia borealis*, *Cochleria fenestrata*, *Saxifraga lamentiniana*, *Poa arctica*, and another undetermined grass, *Hepatica*, a moss, and red lichen covering the rocks. [EDITOR.]

and westward to be a close-grained clay slate, cleaving freely into thin flakes, with here and there a few compact, metamorphic masses that rise above the general surface. Where it is exposed along the shore bluffs and kept bare of vegetation and soil by the action of the ocean, ice, and heavy snow-drifts, the rock presents a surface about as black as coal, without even a moss or lichen to enliven its somber gloom. But when this dreary barrier is passed the surface features of the country in general are found to be finely moulded and collocated, smooth valleys, wide as compared with their depth, trending back from the shore to a range of mountains that appear blue in the distance, and round-topped hills, with their side curves finely drawn, touching and blending in beautiful groups, while scarce a single rock-pile is seen or sheer-walled bluff to break the general smoothness.

The soil has evidently been derived mostly from the underlying slates, though a few fragmentary wasting moraines were observed, containing traveled boulders of quartz and granite which doubtless were brought from the mountains of the interior by glaciers that have recently vanished—so recently that the outlines and sculptured hollows and grooves of the mountains have not as yet suffered sufficient post-glacial denudation to mar appreciably their glacial characters.

The banks of the river at the mouth of which we landed presented a striking contrast as to vegetation to that of any other stream we had seen in the Arctic regions. The tundra vegetation was not wholly absent, but the mosses and lichens of which it is elsewhere composed are about as feebly developed as possible, and instead of forming a continuous covering they occur in small separate tufts, leaving the ground between them raw and bare as that of a newly ploughed field. The phanerogamous plants, both on the lowest grounds and on the slopes and hilltops as far as seen, were in the same severely repressed condition, and as sparsely planted in tufts an inch or two in diameter, with from one to three feet of naked soil between them. Some portions of the coast, however, farther

Appendix

south, presented a greenish hue as seen from the ship at a distance of eight
or ten miles, owing no doubt to vegetation growing under less unfavorable
conditions.

From an area of about half a square mile the following plants were
collected:

Gymnandra Stelleri, Cham. &
   Schlecht.
Poa arctica, R. Br.
Aira cæspitosa, L., var.
   arctica.
Alopecurus alpinus, Sm.
Luzula hyperborea, R. Br.
Stellaria longipes, Goldie, var.
   Edwardsii, T. & G.
Cerastium alpinum, L.
Anemone parviflora, Michx.
Papaver nudicaule, L.
Draba alpina, L.
Cochlearia officinalis, L.
Saxifraga flagellaris, Willd.
Saxifraga stellaris, L., var.
   comosa, Poir.

Saxifraga sileniflora, (Hook.),
   Sternb.
Saxifraga hieracifolia, Waldst. &
   Kit.
Saxifraga rivularis, L., var.,
   hyperborea, Hook.
Saxifraga rivularis, L., var.
   hyperborea, Hook.
Saxifraga bronchialis, L.
Saxifraga serpyllifolia, Pursh.
Potentilla nivea, L.
Potentilla frigida, Vill.? [1]
Armeria macrocarpa, Pursh.
Armeria vulgaris, Willd.
Artemisia borealis, (Pall.), Willd.
Nardosmia frigida, Hook.
Saussurea monticola, Richards.

[1] "*Potentilla emarginata*, Pursh. A very dwarf form of this species from Wrangell
Land was inadvertently named *Potentilla frigida* in the list of Muir's collection."
(Note by Asa Gray in House Executive Document No. 44 (1884–85), p. 191.)
[EDITOR.]

Index

Index

Index

Index

Index

Index

Index